OAK ISLAND
GOLD

William S. Crooker

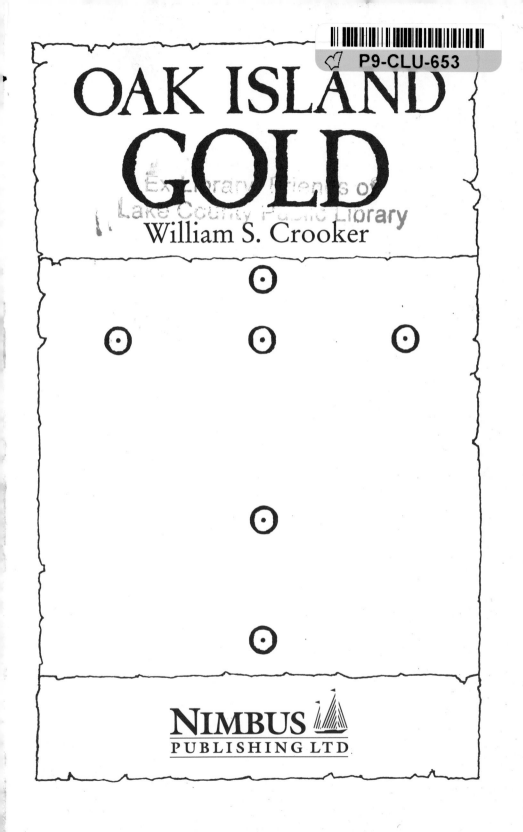

NIMBUS
PUBLISHING LTD

95 96 97   6 5 4

Nimbus Publishing Limited
P.O. Box 9301, Station A
Halifax, N.S. B3K 5N5
(902)-455-4286

Design: Arthur B. Carter, Halifax
Text editor: Andrew Safer

Diagrams were prepared by, and remain the property of, W.S. Crooker, and W.S. Crooker and Associates Ltd., Halifax, N.S.

Printed and bound in Canada

Nimbus Publishing acknowledges the financial support of the Department of Communications and The Canada Council.

Canadian Cataloguing in Publication Data

Crooker, William S.

Oak Island gold
Includes bibliographical references.
ISBN 1-55109-049-X

1. Oak Island treasure site (N.S.) I. Title.
FC2345.035C76 1993   971.6'23   C93-098610-5
F1039.035C76 1993

For my wife, Joan

Acknowledgements

A special acknowledgment is due to the following people for their kind assistance in providing valuable information necessary for the production of this book. Alphabetically they are:

Dan Blankenship, Triton Alliance Project Manager

Joseph Judge, Retired Senior Associate Editor of the *National Geographic Magazine*

Dr. Lian Kieser, Ph.D., Interstate Laboratory, Toronto, Ontario

Harold Krueger, Krueger Enterprises, Inc., Geochron Laboratories Division, Cambridge Massachusetts

Graham McBride, Maritime Museum of the Atlantic, Halifax, Nova Scotia

Frederick G. Nolan, Nova Scotia Land Surveyor

Edmond Telfer, Research Scientist, Environment Canada

David Tobias, President, Triton Alliance

Tim Whynot, Extension Services Division, Nova Scotia Department of Natural Resources

Thanks also to Andrew Safer, Halifax-based freelance editor and writer, who critiqued and edited the manuscript.

Contents

Preface

Before 1958, Oak Island was a well-kept secret. Its legacy was confined to miscellaneous newspaper and magazine articles, the prospectuses of treasure search companies, and isolated chapters of a few books on buried treasure—all scattered over a period of about 100 years. Then, in 1958, *The Oak Island Mystery* was published. In it, Reginald V. Harris related the history of Island activity since 1795, when the first search began. An attorney, Harris had represented two Oak Island treasure hunters. The book is definitive historically, but has its limitations. It leaves many questions unanswered, such as: Who constructed the labyrinth of shafts and tunnels? When was it done? Why was it done? How was it done? These questions have captured my imagination for many years.

A year prior to the release of Harris' book, I had been an engineering student and survey party chief on a highway construction project several miles north of Oak Island. During a mid-morning coffee break, I overheard the men in my crew talking about a nearby island where people were digging for an enormous treasure. It was another Fort Knox and it was there for the taking, if anyone could get to it. The men talked excitedly about an unimaginable quantity of gold buried deep beneath the island, protected by a labyrinth of shafts and tunnels connected to the ocean. Every time treasure hunters had dug within reach of the cache, they had been driven out by a flood of water from the sea. After first hearing the story and later reading Harris' book, I began to follow newspaper accounts of the ongoing treasure searches. This is how I became involved.

In 1972, I took my boat *The Scotia Lass* on my first ocean cruise to Mahone Bay, where Oak Island is situated. Subsequently, I made annual excursions to cruise the waters of the bay in search of clues. I reported my findings in *The Oak Island Quest*, which was published in 1978.

The Oak Island Quest outlines the history of the hunt up to 1978 and it covers most of the theories and speculations of investigators and writers of the day. Some of the speculations I offered were "tongue-in-cheek"—advanced in the interests of not limiting the possibilities, as opposed to representing any firm convictions on my part. The reader is left to reject what he or she feels is too "far-out" to consider.

After writing *The Oak Island Quest*, I have continued to follow the Island's saga as it has unfolded, and in 1991 I began to write *Oak Island Gold*.

While I was still outlining *Oak Island Gold*, one of the Island's current treasure hunters emerged out of the blue to disclose a startling discovery. He then engaged me to conduct an engineering survey. My work on the Island in connection with this find led me to an entirely new path of inquiry. This, in turn, led to the formulation of a novel theory, different from any that had come before. Although I began the relatively straightforward task of chronicling an update of the treasure hunt, I ended up with far more than I had bargained for.

Since a treasure has yet to be recovered, I cannot profess to have solved the mystery, once and for all. Although circumstantial evidence abounds, the irrefutable proof is still in the proverbial pudding.

Perhaps the details of this unexpected survey will spark you to become engaged in the quest—either as an armchair philosopher or as a digger. Perhaps these findings will bring us all one step closer to discovering the irrefutable proof that still eludes our grasp.

W.S.C.

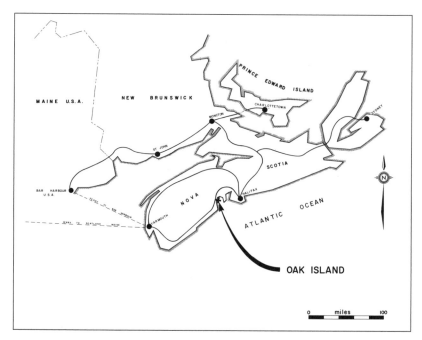

Map of Maritime Provinces and Maine showing location of Oak Island.

ONE

The Mystery Begins

June 17, 1992. Frederick G. Nolan, Nova Scotia Land Surveyor, slowly unzipped a black briefcase and gave me a cryptic smile. We were seated at a corner table in a popular coffee shop overlooking Halifax Harbour. The last rays of a scarlet sunset reflected off the glossy surface of a color photograph being pushed in my direction. "Take a look at this," Nolan said, "and tell me what you see."

A practicing professional surveyor of Bedford, Nova Scotia, Nolan owns a portion of Oak Island, site of the two-century-old treasure hunt that has baffled scores of treasure seekers. Nolan has been involved in the search for over 30 years. Like a man manacled to an obsession he has surveyed, drilled, and dug. I had an intuitive feeling that the photo was going to lead me to a place where only he had ventured. My intuition was correct.

The photo was of a large sandstone boulder about four feet in diameter, displaying a gruesome appearance.

"What do you make of it?" Nolan asked. "Do you notice anything peculiar?"

1

I was reluctant to say. Feeling certain that what the photograph suggested was simply a coincidence, I disregarded my first thought and searched for something else. Finally, after examining the photograph for a couple of minutes, I gave in to an impulse to shun my dignity and blurted, "It looks like a human skull!"

Nolan quickly glanced around the room as if checking to see if I had caught anyone's attention and replied almost in a whisper, "You've got it. That's what it is!"

In the months to follow, the rock-shaped skull which Nolan has dubbed "the Head Stone" would add a bizarre twist to Oak Island's baffling mystery. A mystery that began a very long time ago with the confession of a dying sailor and a lost treasure.

According to legend, in the 1600s an old man on his deathbed, in what was then known as the New England Colonies, said he had been a crew member of the notorious Captain William Kidd. He swore that many years earlier he had assisted Kidd and his crew in burying an enormous treasure on a secluded island east of Boston. The legend was widely spread and early settlers brought the broadly-publicized tale to Nova Scotia. For a century following the alleged confession numerous searches were made, but the treasure was never found.

Then, one day in the late spring or early summer of 1795, a young man, Daniel McGinnis, stumbled upon what he and others became certain was the hiding place of the lost treasure of Captain Kidd.

McGinnis was exploring the eastern end of Oak Island, off the coast of Nova Scotia, when he discovered a spot that appeared to have been worked many years earlier. Someone had cut away a portion of the forest, forming a small clearing in which oak stumps were visible among a new growth of trees. A large forked limb extended over the clearing from one of the original oaks. An old tackle block was attached to the forked part of the limb by means of a wooden peg that connected the fork into a small triangle. The peg, or "treenail" was of a type used in the construction of wooden ships. The ground below the tackle block had settled into a saucer shaped depression about 13 feet in diameter.

The waters off the northeastern coast of North America from Brazil to Newfoundland had once been infested with pirates. LaHave, 15 miles south of Oak Island at the entrance to Mahone Bay, was a depot for pirates in the early 1700s—a depot to which they resorted in great numbers. As one might well imagine, Mahone Bay—in which Oak Island is situated—was a pirate haven.

Having undoubtedly heard the stories of pirate activity in Mahone Bay and the legend of the treasure of Captain Kidd, McGinnis immediately suspected a buried treasure. Enthusiastically, he confided in a couple of close friends: John Smith, age 19, and Anthony Vaughan, age 16. The next day the three of them rushed off to the old clearing.

The tackle block was the foremost point of interest. They immediately climbed up on the limb, but as they tried to remove it, it fell to the ground and broke to smithereens. So they began to investigate the old clearing. Searching about the area, they discovered the remains of a road running from the tree to the western end of the island which gave them hope that the lost treasure of Captain Kidd might be here.

Abandoning further investigation, they hurried back to their homes and returned armed with axes, picks and shovels to begin work with a fervor. They cut away the young trees and began excavating the surface soil. Two feet down they uncovered a layer of carefully laid flagstones. The stones were of a type not found on the island and they figured that they had been transported from Gold River, about two miles north of the island on the mainland.

Once they had removed the flagstones, they found that they were entering the mouth of an old pit or shaft that had been refilled. Although the sides of the shaft were of tough hard clay, the material being removed was loose and easily shoveled without the use of picks, but they noticed pick marks on the sides of the shaft as they shoveled downward.

Pirates had a reputation for being lazy, and it was common knowledge that they buried their treasures only a few feet underground for easy retrieval. Therefore, McGinnis, Smith, and Vaughan expected to hit the top of a wooden chest each time their shovels bit into the soil. By the time they had reached a depth of six or seven feet, they became apprehensive. But treasure fever had set in, and the dig continued downward.

At a depth of ten feet, one of the shovels hit wood. First they were elated, figuring they had hit the cask. But disappointment immediately followed. What they had struck was a platform of oak logs and not the top of a treasure chest.

The ends of the logs that made up the platform were securely embedded into the sides of the shaft. The outside of the logs were rotten, indicating that they had been there for a long time.

The trio probably expected to find a treasure chest directly below the platform but when they removed the logs they found nothing—only a two-foot depression caused by soil settlement. But, again treasure fever got the best of them and they continued to dig downward, day after day. Finally, at a depth of 25 feet, the work became too heavy and they were forced to abandon the dig.

At this point, McGinnis, Smith, and Vaughan realized that someone must have concealed something of extreme value to have gone to the trouble of digging deeper than 25 feet. Disappointed but undaunted, they began to prepare for future work, when help might be available. Before leaving on the final day, they drove wooden sticks into the sides

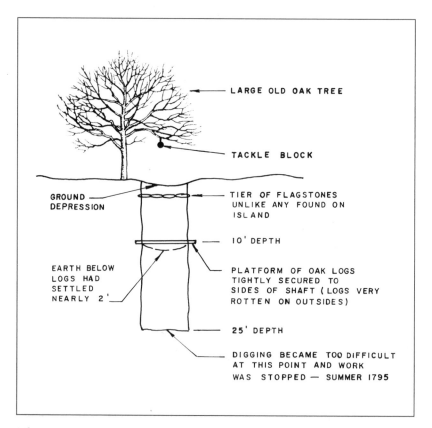

The Money Pit, 1795.

of the pit at the bottom and they covered the place over with trees and brush.

On June 26, 1795, John Smith purchased Lot No. 18 which contained the Money Pit. Eventually, he built a house near the Pit and purchased Lots 15, 16, 17, 19, and 20, making him sole owner of the eastern-most 24 acre portion of the Island.

Maritimers frequently comment after travelling abroad that Nova Scotia is Canada's best-kept secret. The highlands of Cape Breton and the waters of Bras d'Or Lake are unparalleled in their magnificence but they in no way exceed the beauty of the sparkling waters of Mahone Bay, speckled with its numerous sand beach islands.

Oak Island is a small peanut-shaped island hidden from the open sea by many of these spectacular islands. On a gorgeous summer day, one doesn't get the feeling that this island is veiled in the mist of an ancient secret. But Oak Island can take on a sinister appearance when fog rolls in from the Atlantic Ocean and rain and hail pummel her shores. The elegant setting can rapidly become morose and on these occasions one can picture scenes of bloodshed, torture, and torment.

Oak Island is situated about 40 miles south of Halifax and is one of more than 300 islands scattered about Mahone Bay on Nova Scotia's Atlantic coast. It is about three-quarters of a mile in length by 1,000 feet wide at the narrowest section near the center. The long portion of the island runs in an east to west direction with a small crescent-shaped bay called Smith's Cove or Smuggler's Cove situated on the north side at the extreme eastern end. The west end of the Island is linked to Crandall's Point on the mainland by a narrow causeway constructed in 1965 to transport heavy treasure digging equipment. Two roads lead to the Money Pit from the western end of the Island—an old road on the north side and a recently constructed one on the south. For almost two centuries, thousands of people have walked the old road to witness the strange works, hear stories of the digs, and ponder the mystery. The Island, named for the beautiful groves of oaks that once shrouded the hills, is now mostly covered with scrub and spruce trees. The east end is sparsely vegetated and severely pocked and scarred from decades of digging for the elusive treasure.

Topographically, the Island consists of two oval shaped hills about 30 feet high separated by a swamp and marshy area over the narrow

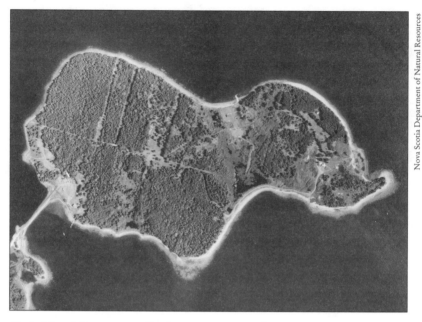

Oak Island from one mile above; 1992 aerial mapping.

Causeway constructed in 1965 to admit a huge excavating machine, used to dig for treasure.

section. Many investigators of the Oak Island mystery, including Fred Nolan who owns land on that portion of the island, believe that the swamp is associated somehow with the legendary treasure.

The soil of the Island is a hard-stiff clay more than 100 feet deep, overlying a bedrock of limestone. Deep within the limestone formation, present searchers have found what they believe is evidence of man-made workings.

Smith's Cove has a very unusual feature. Its beach is artificial! Sometime, long ago, before the discovery of the Money Pit, it was made by man.

The mysterious Money Pit lies near the top of the high oval shaped hill on the east end of the Island, 500 feet from the shore of Smith's Cove. And here, for the past 200 years, men have wasted fortunes and lost their lives in search of buried booty.

Daniel McGinnis, the discoverer of the Money Pit, is himself an enigma. No one knows where he came from or where he lived. His age in 1795 is unknown. His origin and parentage is unknown. However, we do know a bit about Anthony Vaughan and John Smith. Perhaps from their origins and lineages we can read between the lines and make a good guess about the man named Daniel McGinnis.

On October 18, 1759, Nova Scotia's British Governor-in-Chief, Charles Lawrence, granted 100,000 acres of Crown land known as the "Shoreham Grant" to about 76 immigrants from the British colony of New England. This grant included the township of Shoreham which is now Chester, the area which is now a community known as the Western Shore, and several Mahone Bay islands, including Oak Island. An additional grant of 29,750 acres was made in 1760 and another of 12,400 acres in 1785.

Most of Oak Island was granted to New England families but none are known to have had the names of McGinnis, Smith, or Vaughan.

But on March 8, 1768, an Edward Smith acquired title to Lot 19, adjacent to Lot 18 which contains the Money Pit, and John Smith's father who may have been a relative of Edward's probably settled on the Island. According to M. B. DesBrisay in his History of the County of Lunenburg (Nova Scotia) [1895 edition], John Smith was born on August 20, 1775 and died on Oak Island on September 29, 1857 after living there 71 years. In view of these dates and his term of residency on

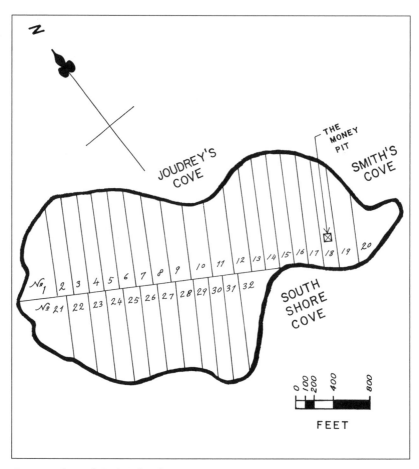

Survey plan of Oak Island.

the Island, it appears that he moved there in 1786 at the age of 11.

Anthony Vaughan's father immigrated from Massachusetts in 1772 and acquired 200 acres of land on the mainland near Oak Island which is now the community known as the "Western Shore." He was one of three brothers who settled in the Chester area. One of his brothers, Daniel, acquired title to Lots 13 and 14, three lots removed from the Money Pit Lot No. 18.

There is no record of Daniel McGinnis' family having owned land on Oak Island or on the mainland prior to 1795. DesBrisay writes, "The first settlers were John McMullen and Daniel McInnis [McGinnis]" and states that three men, Smith, McGinnis, and Vaughan, emigrated from New England to Chester and that Smith and McGinnis settled on Oak Island and Vaughan on the mainland. DesBrisay was probably referring to the fathers of the discoverers because as noted above, Anthony Vaughan's father had acquired 200 acres on the mainland near Oak Island in 1772. Also, John Smith was too young to have "settled" at the age of 11.

We may glean from DesBrisay's accounts therefore, that in 1795 when the Money Pit was discovered, Anthony Vaughan was living on the mainland, John Smith on the Island and quite possibly so was Daniel McGinnis.

So, in the year 1795, three young men who in all probability were neighbors as well as close friends became involved in an enigma that would consume their lives and ensnare the lives of their children and their children's children. They had launched a saga that would claim lives and squander fortunes.

TWO

Thwarted

After the discovery and excavation of the Money Pit down to a depth of 25 feet, almost a decade elapsed before the dig was resumed.

It is assumed that Daniel McGinnis and his companions John Smith and Anthony Vaughan initially failed to acquire help to continue the dig due to local superstition about Oak Island, and the lack of free time available to the hard working men of the area.

Many years before the discovery of the Money Pit, the people of Chester, three miles across the Bay, noticed strange lights glowing on Oak Island at night. Fishermen ventured as close as they dared and observed what appeared to be pirates silhouetted against huge bonfires. Curiosity grew and two men went out to the Island to investigate. They never returned and were not heard from or seen again. That is the story as it was handed down. The tale is said to have been revealed by an old woman in Chester when the Money Pit was discovered. The story had been related to her many years before by her grandmother. Added to this tale were the superstitious beliefs that witches frequented the Island and that ghosts of victims buried with booty guard a pirate treasure.

Most of the inhabitants of the Chester area were poor hard-working farmers and fishermen with little leisure time. Their only salvation from day to day drudgery was their adhesion to religious traditions that included the observation of Sunday as a day of rest. It was a day on which any kind of work for financial gain or subsistence was forbidden—including digging for pirate treasure.

But, was it really superstition and lack of available manpower that stopped the discoverers from continuing the dig? It doesn't seem credible that the hardy settlers wouldn't have braved the ghosts and gambled a few days or weeks of fishing or farming for a fortune in gold. It seems more probable that McGinnis, Smith, and Vaughan made a pact to keep the Money Pit a secret until they could find financial assistance to continue the search.

The discoverers probably felt a strong need to protect their find. They may have asked themselves, "What will happen if we go through the community talking about everything we've found and asking for help? Is it possible that a group of men from Chester might invade the Island?" I certainly would have held such a concern. The discoverers were probably not unlike the present searchers with regard to the matter of secrecy. Fred Nolan, one of the searchers previously mentioned, once told me that "secrecy" is of the utmost importance to him and his neighbor treasure searchers and expressed his annoyance about someone who had recently trespassed on his Oak Island property.

The discoverers needed a financial backer. Like their Chester neighbors, they were poor hard-working fishermen and farmers. Without financial help, how could they raise the money to pay the wages of laborers. They were sure of uncovering an enormous treasure and undoubtedly didn't want to have to split it among a group of hired men, in lieu of a few days or weeks of manual labor.

In the years following the discovery, Daniel McGinnis married and began farming the southwestern end of the Island. Anthony Vaughan married and settled on the mainland near the Island in the neighborhood now known as the Western Shore. John Smith, who was married in 1790, five years before the discovery, built a house near the Money Pit and began farming the eastern end of the Island.

So, it was easy for Daniel McGinnis and his partners to watch over the Money Pit while they searched for a backer.

Early accounts differ as to when that backer was eventually found. DesBrisay's account gives fifteen years after the discovery and other accounts say it was seven years. Fifteen years seems like a rather long time, considering the riches they expected. The evidence indicates that seven years or 1802 is probably correct.

The backer was a gentleman of financial status from Onslow, near Truro, at the head of the Bay of Fundy, Nova Scotia, by the name of Simeon Lynds. He was related to Anthony Vaughan's father.

There are two versions of the first Oak Island financier. One account refers to Simeon Lynds as Dr. Lynds from Truro and says that his involvement came about because John Smith's wife, Sarah, refused to have her first child on Oak Island because of the superstition connected with the Money Pit. She travelled to Truro, a distance of more than 100 miles overland, and had her baby delivered by Dr. Lynds. Smith accompanied her and took the doctor into his confidence, intending to win him as a financial backer. Lynds was intrigued with Smith's story and returned with the Smiths to Oak Island. After seeing the Money Pit, Dr. Lynds returned to Truro and formed a company to go after the treasure.

It seems unlikely that Smith's wife would journey all the way to Truro to have a baby, considering the extreme hardship posed by the difficulty of travel in those days. If there wasn't a physician in Chester, there were most certainly experienced midwives. This version of the story is further weakened by the fact that John, the Smith's first child, was christened at Chester on April 15, 1798, four years before Lynds visited Oak Island.

According to a more plausible version, Simeon Lynds was on business in Chester and spent an evening with Anthony Vaughan's father. During the course of the evening's conversation, Lynds heard about the discovery. The next day Lynds went over to the Island with Vaughan to see the Money Pit.

Lynds was apparently carried away by what he saw and heard, for he returned home and formed the Onslow Company in order to attract investors to provide the necessary funds to hire men and equipment to continue the excavation of the Money Pit. He appointed Colonel Robert Archibald director of operations and the company was successful in attracting over two dozen substantial investors from the Onslow and Truro regions. They were friends of Lynds and in addition to Colonel Archibald included such prominent men as Sheriff Thomas Harris of Pictou and Captain David Archibald who were men of substantial standing in their communities.

Colonel Archibald was a surveyor who laid out the Township of Onslow in 1780. He was also Justice of the Peace and Town Clerk for the area that is now Pictou and Colchester Counties. It is noteworthy that men of Archibald's caliber were among the first to become involved in the Oak Island treasure hunt.

The winter and spring of 1803 must have passed very slowly for McGinnis, Smith, Vaughan, and their wives. The Lynds party had made plans to start work that summer. One can imagine the long restless nights filled with dreams about bushels of gold and silver coins and the excitement that must have flared up when the families would meet on occasion to discuss the upcoming search.

For the men, a share of the expected treasure may have meant freedom from a lifetime of toil, a couple of fine horses, a luxurious carriage, or a new sloop. For the ladies, the treasure may have offered freedom from household drudgery, salvation from tending the live-stock and working in the vegetable garden, the promise of fine china dishes, silver culinary, silk dresses, an education for their children in Europe, and a luxurious home in the town of Chester.

So, the early discoverers and their wives anxiously waited while the Onslow company completed their arrangements and put their plans into motion.

In the summer of 1803, the newly-found syndicate loaded up a boat at Onslow with supplies and equipment and set sail for Oak Island. Their course took them southwesterly to the mouth of the Bay of Fundy, counterclockwise around the southwestern end of the Province and northeasterly to Mahone Bay, a distance of about 350 miles.

McGinnis, Smith, and Vaughan joined the Lynds party on arrival and introduced them to the old pit.

Work in the outset was not as easy as Colonel Archibald and Lynds had expected. Since the work halted in 1795, the Pit had caved in and the first task was to clean out the mud and debris. The crew completed this chore with some difficulty, but they were delighted to find the sticks that the three discoverers had driven into the mud to mark their final digging spot. The presence of the sticks confirmed that no one had tampered with the site during the eight-year lapse.

Driving downward beyond where McGinnis and his companions had quit, a shovel eventually struck wood. Expectations undoubtedly soared but when the crew removed more soil all they found was another tier of logs comprising an oak platform similar to the one encountered in 1795.

Ten feet further down they came upon a layer of charcoal, ten feet lower a layer of putty, and much further down a most enigmatic object. It was a flagstone that bore mysterious letters and figures. The stone was about 24 inches long by 16 inches wide and it was found with the figures facing downward. No one in the search party could decipher the stone etchings so it was temporarily cast aside. That strange piece of rock later became one of the most talked-about artifacts of all—the center of enormous controversy and speculation.

Some of the old accounts say that platforms of oak were struck at the 10, 20 and 30-foot levels and if so, the charcoal and putty would have then been situated at the 40-foot and 50-foot levels respectively. However, there are minor variations in the early accounts. According to Reginald V. Harris, author of *The Oak Island Mystery*, one account says that the putty was found at the 40-foot level, spread over a log platform, and that there was so much of it that it provided glazing for the windows of more than 20 houses in Mahone Bay. Further, it said that the charcoal was found at the 50-foot level along with more oak planks. After the planks were removed, ten feet further down, coconut fiber was discovered and again another platform of oak.

James McNutt, who worked on the Island in 1863, states, "At 40 feet a tier of charcoal; at 50 feet a tier of smooth stones from the beach, with figures and letters cut on them; at 60 feet a tier of manilla grass and the rind of the coconut; at 70 feet a tier of putty; at 80 feet a stone three feet long and one foot square, with figures and letters cut on it, and being freestone, being different from any on that coast." Adams A. Tupper who worked on the dig in the summers of 1850, 1851 and 1863 gives an account which places the inscribed stone at 90 feet but makes no mention of the putty, charcoal, or coconut fiber. Reginald V. Harris says that quantities of coconut fiber were removed from the Pit from

No. 5

THIS ENVELOPE CONTAINS A SAMPLE OF THE
ANCIENT COCONUT FIBRE TAKEN FROM THE
TREASURE-PIT ON OAK ISLAND, NOVA SCOTIA.
ITS PRESENCE THERE WOULD SEEM TO INDICATE
A TROPICAL ORIGIN FOR THE TREASURE, WHICH
TO OUR MIND ALMOST CERTAINLY CAME FROM
SOMEWHERE AROUND THE CARIBBEAN.

Sample of coconut fiber taken from the Money Pit.

time to time, and Hiram Walker, a ship carpenter who had worked with
the early searchers, told his granddaughter, Mrs. Cottnam Smith, that
he had seen bushels of coconut fiber brought up from the Money Pit.

No water had been encountered until the 90-foot level was reached. At
this depth the bottom of the pit became soggy and water began to ooze
from the clay. At 93 feet, water intrusion became a nuisance. The crew

found themselves removing one bucket of water for every two of soil. With the dusk of night approaching, the men probed the mushy bottom of the pit with a crowbar to see if they could strike anything below. This was their standard practice every evening before dark and on this evening, five feet below the bottom of the pit, at a depth of 98 feet, the bar struck a hard, impenetrable material bounded by the sides of the pit.

The searchers suspected that they had finally encountered Captain Kidd's treasure and the men returned home in high spirits. The fact that a considerable amount of water was seeping in at the bottom of the Pit may have weighted their expectations in favor of a treasure cask rather than another platform of logs. How could the treasure have been placed much deeper considering the amount of water flowing into the Pit?

If Daniel McGinnis and his companions had spent a winter and spring of restless nights, the night following the probe of what seemed most likely to be the treasure chest must have been one of no sleep at all. This had to be the end of the search. Could Kidd have possibly gone any deeper? The treasure seemed just within their grasp.

But when the searchers returned to the Pit the next morning, they were shocked by what lay below. The shaft, which had remained dry throughout all the previous weeks, was now filled with about 60 feet of water.

Discouraged but undaunted, the crew dug in their heels and began bailing out the pit with buckets. They bailed day and night before conceding that their work was useless. Despite their considerable efforts, the water in the shaft remained at the same level.

As it was approaching haying season and some of the men had to return home to cut, dry and store their grass, Colonel Archibald temporarily halted the work. That fall, a committee was sent to see a Mr. Mosher of Newport, Hants County, Nova Scotia, who was considered to be the best person in the province to consult regarding how to remove the water. The Company paid Mr. Mosher 80 pounds to rig up a pump which he lowered to the 90-foot depth in the Pit. He started it up, but the pump burst before the water reached the surface. With winter approaching, Colonel Archibald called off the project until the following year when an alternative plan could be put in place.

The following spring, the Onslow Company returned to Oak Island with redoubled vigor and a new approach to bailing out the Pit.

They sank a shaft 110 feet deep at a point 14 feet southeast of the

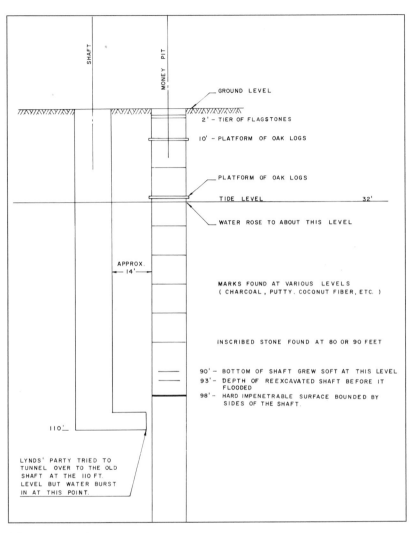

The Money Pit, 1804.

Money Pit. They planned to tunnel in under the bottom of the Money Pit and remove the treasure from below. They didn't encounter any water when they excavated the new shaft, and they started to dig a tunnel from the 110-foot level towards the bottom of the Money Pit. But when the diggers got to within two feet of the old pit, water began to ooze in small streams from the end of the tunnel. The bank between the end of the tunnel and the Money Pit suddenly collapsed, water burst into the tunnel and the workmen barely escaped with their lives. Within two hours, the new shaft was filled to the 65-foot level, equal to the depth of water in the Money Pit.

Further attempts at bailing proved futile. The Onslow Company's funds were now exhausted, and the project was abandoned.

Almost a half century would pass before the next attempt to reach the illusive treasure.

THREE

The Inscribed Stone

For Daniel McGinnis, John Smith, Anthony Vaughan and their spouses, the hope for achieving great wealth had vanished.

Luxurious homes in the town of Chester, fine horses, sailing ships, leisure time, servants, wardrobes filled with expensive clothing, travel to Europe—all that treasure might have bought was lost forever. They had tried for seven years to find a sponsor and to that end they had succeeded. But the efforts of the venturers had ended in failure. News of the defeat spread quickly. It was inconceivable that another backer could be found in light of the Onslow Company's financial disaster. Who would want to invest in a project that stonewalled the likes of Colonel Archibald and Simeon Lynds?

Daniel McGinnis and his companion discoverers could only stand beside the old Pit and gaze down into the murky water. What had happened? What freak of nature had fouled their efforts and undone their days of back-breaking toil?

How had Kidd contended with the water? McGinnis and his companions must have asked. Perhaps he had booby-trapped the Pit. But if so, how?

There had to be a reason for the rush of water that filled the pits and some of the searchers thought the answer was written on that strange stone. The one with the mysterious marks and figures.

The stone had been found at the 80- or 90-foot level (accounts differ) with crude marks and figures engraved on the downward-facing side.

Smith, Vaughan, McGinnis, Simeon Lynds, Colonel Archibald and others had examined the inscription on the stone and pondered its meaning. They could make no sense of the weird marks. What did the stone indicate? Why had it been placed so very far down in the Pit?

They asked each other if, "The stone carried a code of instructions on how to de-water the Pit. Had they been clever enough to decipher the inscription, would all their problems have been avoided?"

Smith was in the process of building a fireplace in his house near the Money Pit. Perhaps for safe-keeping or as a conversation-piece, he placed it in the fireplace jamb.

News of the Money Pit travelled far and wide and people began to visit the Island to satisfy their curiosity. It is said that over many years following the completion of Smith's house, hundreds of people visited the Pit and viewed the strange inscribed stone displayed in Smith's fireplace.

Around 1865, the stone was removed from the fireplace jamb by A.O. Creighton, treasurer of a then newly-formed Oak Island search group, and it was taken to Halifax. It was exhibited in the window of a bookbinders shop (A. and H. Creighton, established in 1844) to help sell shares for the treasure-seeking company.

In 1894, Jefferson W. MacDonald, one of the people who helped remove the stone, told a searcher that the inscription was clearly visible but nobody present was able to decipher it.

The A. and H. Creighton business ended in 1879 with the death or retirement of A.O. Creighton and a new firm was formed by Herbert Creighton of the former bookbinding company, and Edward Marshall. The new company was called Creighton and Marshall which carried on the old bookbinding business.

Edward Marshall's son, Harry, who took up employment with the new firm in 1890, made the following statement to Frederick L. Blair (an Oak Island treasure hunter) and Reginald V. Harris, his lawyer:

"I well remember seeing it as a boy and until the business was merged in 1919 in the present firm of Phillips and Marshall.

"The stone was about two feet long, fifteen inches wide and ten inches thick, and weighed about 175 pounds. It had two smooth surfaces, with rough sides and traces of cement attached to them. Tradition said that it had been part of two fireplaces. The corners were not squared but somewhat rounded. The block resembled dark Swedish granite, or fine grained porphyry, very hard, and with an olive tinge, and did not resemble any local Nova Scotia stone. While in Creighton's possession some one had cut his initials 'J.M.' on one corner, but apart from this there was no evidence of any inscription either cut or painted on the stone. It had completely faded out. We used the stone for a beating stone and weight.

"When the business was closed in 1919, Thomas Forhan, since deceased, asked for the stone, the history of which seems to have been generally known. When we left the premises in 1919 the stone was left behind, but Forhan does not seem to have taken it. Search at Forhan's business premises and residence two years ago (1933) disclosed no stone.

"Thorough searches of the old premises in 1935, and of the stone yards of Brookfield Construction Company on Smith and Mitchell Streets, Halifax, have failed to discover the stone."

A presumed copy of the marks and figures found on the stone is given in a book by Edward Rowe Snow entitled *True Tales of Buried Treasure*, published in 1962. According to Snow, a Reverend A.T. Kempton of Cambridge, Massachusetts, claimed that an old Irish schoolmaster had deciphered the code as, "Forty feet below two million pounds are buried."

According to rumor, another deciphering of the stone's inscription was made by a Dalhousie University language professor, James Liechti. The translation complies with that given by the Irish schoolmaster with the exception that it reads: "Ten feet below two million pounds lie buried." One is compelled to question why a message would be placed above a treasure with complete information on its vertical location and exact value in pounds. If the originators of the Money Pit required a vertical benchmark and statement of value, surely they would have left something less than a coded message.

A logical approach would have been to place a stone with a simple "x" mark on its surface and memorize or record its meaning without reference to Mahone Bay and Oak Island. To go one step further, it is reasonable to question why any mark at all would have been required on the stone. The placement of a 175-pound boulder far down in the Pit should have been more than sufficient with reference to a memorized or recorded message.

If we choose to believe that the inscription may have been a message that had no bearing on the location of a treasure, what was the real purpose of the inscribed stone?

For a very long time, investigators of the Oak Island mystery have contended that the inscription is a code of instructions on how to shut off the water in the Money Pit. And some enthusiasts believe that the inscription as we know it is part of a complex mathematical equation which is required to match wits with the unknown designer.

I have long pondered the concept that the inscription is an important piece of the puzzle and welcomed a letter received in 1980 from a woman in Alberta, Canada, who wrote that the engraving on the stone may have an astrological interpretation. She had watched a television documentary on the program "The Fifth Estate" and was left with the impression that some of the symbols were astrological. She acquired a copy of my book *The Oak Island Quest*, analyzed the inscription, enclosed her interpretation of some of the figures, and suggested that I consult an astrologer in my area to help with further deciphering. The letter lay dormant in my files until this book was well underway and I remembered the correspondence. On checking her interpretation of the symbols, I could make no sense whatsoever of their meaning and met with a well-known and respected astrologer, as the writer had suggested, but the results were negative. The astrologer identified some of the symbols as astrological but was unable to decode the inscription.

Then I recalled reading that Joseph R. Judge, retired senior associate editor of the *National Geographic Magazine*, had made an identical translation, in 1987, of the inscription given in Snow's book. I wrote him for information. He replied that he recalled decoding the inscription but couldn't remember the contents of the message with any exactitude except that it was "a ridiculously easy 'code,' such as numbering letters, A being 1 and B 2 etc." He recalled the message said "something like, 'Dig down ten feet and find the treasure.' "

I found Judge's statement that the inscription was easy to decode

Inscription written on stone found at 80- or 90-foot level.

most intriguing and tried my own hand at the game. I took the inscription and applied the symbols as decoded to the English alphabet and got nowhere. I then checked my dictionary and found that a few of the symbols matched those in the Greek, Hebrew, and Cyrillic alphabets but to such a limited extent as to be meaningless to me. I gave up and sent Judge a copy of the inscription along with a letter asking if it had been written with code symbols well-known in the early 1900s and suggested that, if so, possibly it had been faked by a member of a treasure seeking company and given to an unsuspecting scholar to decode.

Judge replied in a letter dated August 1, 1992. He said, "I recognized the inscription when I saw it again. You will see immediately that it is rendered in the simplest geometric forms—crosses, circles, squares, triangles, dots. The forms derived from these are endless but also simple. Whoever made the inscription using these basic symbols probably left a simple message as well, something like 'Dig…' and the presence of two three-letter words indicated it was probably in English and these words were 'the' or 'are.' "

Judge explained his deciphering system: "I simply applied Poe's system from *The Gold Bug* in which he gives the most fundamental of all decipherment rules, that the symbol appearing most frequently will be an 'E' since it is the most frequently occurring letter in English. The most frequent symbol here is one of two dots stacked vertically, thus the second word is blank-e-e-blank. In a buried treasure inscription that can only be 'feet' and once that is known the ballgame is over. You have the F and T of 'FORTY' which then gives you O, R and Y. And FORTY FEET blank-E-blank-O-blank can be guessed out as BELOW at once. The rest is just working from known letters as they become known."

Judge suggested that I might be interested in the complete list of frequent letters from Poe's story and gave E as the most common followed by A O I D H N R S T U Y C F G L M W B K P Q X Z. Judge then went on to write, "There does not seem to be an internal order in the encoded alphabet, although there is a hint of one in the symbols chosen for the vowels—a single dot for A, two for E, three for I, two separated by a slash for O—but then a cross instead of four dots for U. The series P-R-S uses circles, so a good guess would be the missing Q is also a circle, probably with a NW–SE line through it. The whole thing is rather childish, like something from a Boy Scout Manual. The words are even separated, making deciphering a comparative cinch."

Obviously, the inscription as we know it today is a hoax—a modern invention deliberately made simple to lure potential investors. It is highly unlikely that the originators of the Money Pit left a coded message giving the amount and depth of buried treasure.

Judge justifiably presumes that the intelligence that constructed the Money Pit would have "devised a far more sophisticated method and message." Furthermore, he contends that the idiom seems to be 20th century as the figure of "two million of anything" is of a modern scale.

But the stone and an inscription *did* exist. It is mentioned in all the early accounts of the Onslow company's expedition.

The stone may have been a clue on how to shut off the water or, indeed, it may have contained the key to unlock the Oak Island mystery. But we will never know unless a true copy of the stone's engraving is found. And, hopefully, that will happen.

It is only reasonable to presume that out of the hundreds of people who viewed the inscribed stone, many copied down the symbols. Curiosity and the challenge of a puzzle must have driven people to copy or trace the marks and figures. Perhaps somewhere in someone's personal archives a copy of the real inscription lays hidden, and will someday be revealed.

FOUR

The Discovery of Oak Casks

The Onslow Company's failure to recover Captain Kidd's supposed treasure was followed by a long period of inactivity. The 1804 defeat apparently dampened interest in the Island's prospects and discouraged potential investors.

Simeon Lynds and Colonel Archibald packed up their equipment and returned home to face disappointed and distraught investors. Daniel McGinnis and his companion discoverers abandoned the dream of becoming wealthy gentlemen and returned to fishing and farming for a living.

It was not until 45 years later that another venture was organized. In 1849, a group of Nova Scotia businessmen formed the Truro Company which was named after the town where most of the members lived.

The basic structure of the new company comprised John Gammell of Upper Stewiacke, a large shareholder, Jotham B. McCully of Truro, manager of operations, James Pitblado, mining engineer and foreman, and a Dr. Lynds of Truro, frequently confused with Simeon Lynds of the 1803–1804 project.

Daniel McGinnis didn't live to participate in the new search but John Smith and Anthony Vaughan, both in their seventies, were still alive and they pointed out the location of the old stand to the new party.

John Smith had filled in the old shafts in the intervening years and the first job undertaken was to reexcavate the Money Pit. After about two weeks of work, on a Saturday night, they reached a depth of 86 feet. To their horror, on the way back from church the next day, they discovered 60 feet of water in the Pit. As in 1803, all attempts at bailing failed to lower the water by the slightest amount. According to one account, the operation was "as satisfactory as taking soup with a fork."

History had repeated itself. The adventurers came up against the same phenomenon their predecessors, the Onslow Company, had fought in 1803. The Truro Company had either chosen to ignore the problem, or they thought that the original flooding of the Money Pit had been a fluke of nature, corrected by 45 years.

Failing to bail out the Money Pit, they set about drilling. The exact purpose of the boring operation is not clear from the old accounts. It may well be that they could no longer constrain their curiosity about the treasure, or they needed to determine its value before mounting a new attack. A third possibility is that they may have hoped to suck up the treasure by using drilling procedures. But regardless of the purpose, with the Money Pit two-thirds filled with unbailable water, something had to be done.

They constructed a platform in the Money Pit at the 30-foot level, slightly above the water surface. A primitive drilling apparatus called a pod auger used in prospecting for coal was set up on the platform. The drilling machine was hand-operated. It brought up cores of drilled material by the screwing motion of a chisel-tipped auger (a tool for boring holes in the earth with a sharp end for cutting and spiral grooves for channeling the cuttings out of the hole.)

Five holes were drilled to a depth of 112 feet. While attempting to drill the first hole they lost the only valve sludger (a long podlike container equipped with a valve at the bottom to prevent the contents from dropping out) they had. In a letter to a friend dated June 2, 1862, McCully wrote: "Having lost it [the valve sludger] we had only one left, which had, instead of a valve, a ball inside with a pin across the bottom to keep the ball from dropping out. That one would not admit of coin passing into it. It would seem strange that we would not have got

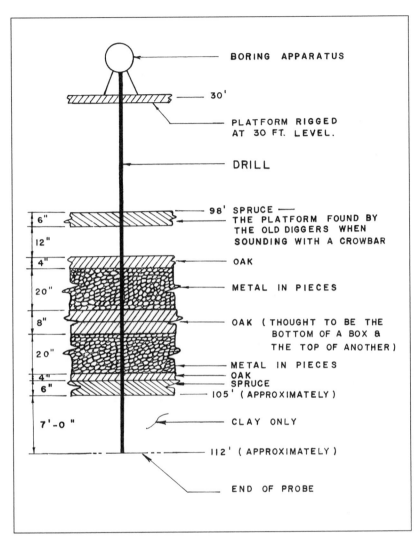

BORING APPARATUS

30'

PLATFORM RIGGED
AT 30 FT. LEVEL.

DRILL

98' SPRUCE —
THE PLATFORM FOUND BY
THE OLD DIGGERS WHEN
SOUNDING WITH A CROWBAR

6"
12"

4"
20"

OAK

METAL IN PIECES

8"

20"

OAK (THOUGHT TO BE THE
BOTTOM OF A BOX &
THE TOP OF ANOTHER)

METAL IN PIECES
OAK
SPRUCE
105' (APPROXIMATELY)

4"
6"

7'-0"

CLAY ONLY

112' (APPROXIMATELY)

END OF PROBE

1849 drilling discovery.

another valve sludger, but people who are penny wise and pound foolish sometimes do strange things. I wanted the persons in charge to send for two or three, but could not prevail on them to do so."

The second hole struck the barrier at the 98-foot level which had been probed by the Onslow Company in 1803. It was found to be five inches thick and made of spruce. Passing through the barrier, the auger dropped twelve inches and then went through four inches of oak, then twenty inches of metal in small pieces, and then eight inches of oak which was thought to be the bottom of one cask and the beginning of another. Then the auger went through another twenty inches of metal, the same as before, then four inches of oak, six inches of spruce, and then seven feet of "worked clay" to hard clay that had never been disturbed. We are told that the sound of the auger passing through the loose metal was distinctly audible.

But the auger failed to bring up any evidence of treasure except three pieces of metal which was thought to resemble links from an ancient watch chain. In the previously mentioned 1862 letter to a friend, McCully described the chain as "three small links which had apparently been forced from an epaulette [a shoulder ornament for a uniform]. They were gold."

They bored another hole and once again encountered the barrier at the 98-foot level. On passing through, they dropped 18 inches further and scraped against the side of a supposed cask.

In a written statement on the drilling operation, McCully said, "The flat chisel revolving close to the side of the cask gave it a jerky and irregular motion. On withdrawing the auger, several splinters of oak, such as might come from the side of an oak stave, and a small quantity of brown fibrous substance, closely resembling the husk of a coconut, were brought up. The distance between the upper and lower platforms was found to be six feet."

Further borings were carried out that added nothing to the collection of evidence, but there is reason to believe that a discovery was concealed. James Pitblado, the mining engineer-foreman, had been instructed to carefully remove and store, for microscopic analysis, every single particle of material brought up by the auger. John Gammell, the shareholder with a substantial interest in the project, was present at the time and stated that he watched Pitblado conceal evidence. According to Gammell, when the engineer thought no one was watching, he removed something from the auger, washed and carefully examined it and then slipped it into his pocket. Gammell demanded to see what Pitblado had found but was refused. Pitblado told him that he would have to wait until the next board meeting when it would be shown to all the directors.

James Pitblado failed to show up at the board of directors meeting and none of his colleagues ever learned what he had removed from the auger.

Pitblado's discovery must have been quite significant. He left the Island immediately on pocketing the object taken from the auger and on August 1, 1849, he and Charles Dickson Archibald, manager of the Acadian Iron Works in Londonderry, Nova Scotia, applied to the Province for a license to dig for treasure on Oak Island. They received the license a short time later, but it limited digging to "ungranted and unoccupied lands." Pitblado and Archibald then tried to purchase the eastern end of the Island where the Money Pit is situated, without success.

Archibald moved to England a few years later. Pitblado is said to have been killed in a gold mine or railway construction accident in 1850 but that information has never been confirmed. (No one has ever come forward with information regarding Pitblado's discovery; perhaps Archibald was the only person who knew what Pitblado had removed from the auger on that summer day of 1849.)

The next summer, in 1850, the Truro Company sank a shaft ten feet northwest of the Money Pit with the intent of reaching the casks by lateral tunneling. One account says that the sole purpose of this shaft was to facilitate bailing but it is more likely that it was primarily dug to reach the casks and failing that, to be used as a pumping shaft to aid in efforts to lower the water level in the Money Pit.

They encountered no water in excavating the new shaft and reached a depth of 109 feet. While tunneling towards the bottom of the casks, the workmen ran for their lives when water suddenly burst into the tunnel and the new shaft filled up with 45 feet of water in 20 minutes.

They attempted to bail out the Money Pit by bailing from both the Pit and the new shaft using two pumping gins, each powered by two horses. (A gin is a machine for hoisting heavy objects such as a tub or barrel filled with water.)

Adams A. Tupper, one of the workmen, states in an account of the operations, "Work was carried on night and day for about a week, but all in vain, the only difference being that with the doubled appliances the water could be kept at a lower level than formerly."

Soon, the Truro Company's work crew learned why the Money Pit could not be bailed dry. In uncovering the reason, they found one of the most amazing pieces of the Oak Island puzzle.

FIVE

The Artificial Beach

Although Jotham McCully, the Truro Company's manager, and his workmen were unable to reach the bottom of the water-filled Money Pit, they now had a well constructed perception of what lay below. It was now clear from the drilling probes that there were two large oak casks, one on top of the other, and that they were filled with loose metal. They thought the metal pieces were probably coin, which had been sunken to a depth of between 98 and 105 feet.

Excitement grew with the discovery of the casks, but the magnitude of the find paled in comparison with the discoveries immediately to follow.

Sometime in 1850, after the flooding of the new shaft, someone in the search party noticed that the water in the shafts was salt and that it rose and fell about 18 inches with the tides. The water levels in the shafts were also seen to correspond with the mean tide level of the Bay.

Pondering the phenomenon, the search party asked, "Why was no water encountered in the shafts excavated in 1804 and again in 1850 until they were connected to the Money Pit by lateral tunneling?" These shafts had both been dug close to the Money Pit in the same extremely hard clay.

It was now obvious that somehow a huge amount of saltwater had entered from the bottom of the Money Pit but not from the bottom of the other shafts. The question was: How? The presence of very hard clay made it unlikely that a natural underground watercourse would run from the Bay to the Pit. And, if a natural channel did exist, how could the originators of the Pit have managed to construct the wooden platforms and deposit the casks? The Truro group was certain that a man-made flood tunnel connected the bottom of the Money Pit with the sea. But from where?

It had long been noticed that a small stream of water flowed out of the bank of the shore at Smith's Cove during low tides. Was this water flow connected to the Money Pit? The team became suspicious of this circumstance, and set about searching the beach. They were astonished to discover that the beach was artificial!

A few minutes of shoveling into the sand and gravel beach exposed a bed of a brown fibrous plant resembling that found in the Money Pit. (It was subsequently proven to be coconut fiber, used in former times as "dunnage" for stowing ship's cargo.) The fiber bed was about two inches thick and covered an area extending 145 feet along the shoreline from just above low to high water marks. Below this and to the same extent, they found four or five inches of decayed eel grass. Underlying the eel grass was a dense mass of beach stones, free from sand and gravel.

To make further investigation possible, they built a cofferdam of rock and clay around the cove to hold back the tides. The idea of building a dam may have been taken from the originators of the Money Pit. Jotham McCully, in his 1862 letter to a friend (mentioned in the previous chapter) ends by remarking, "By the way, the remains of an old dam was seen outside the place where we found the drain and the tunnel at the shore."

Once the project was completed and the area was free of water, they began digging just inside the dam and discovered that the original clay had been removed and replaced with beach stones. Removing a portion of these stones revealed five well constructed box drains resting on the bottom of this excavation. They were constructed of parallel lines of rocks spaced about eight inches apart and covered with flat stones. The entrances of these drains were widely separated along the full length of the excavation at low tide and then converged like the fingers of a hand to a common point near the shore.

The workers set about dismantling the drains, working back towards the shore from the cofferdam. As the work progressed, they noticed that the excavation and drains sloped downward from low water towards the shore. Work continued until they were half-way back to the shore from the dam, where the bottom of the excavation was found to be five feet below the original beach. At this point an unusually high tide overflowed the dam and, as it was not built to resist pressure from inside, it was carried away. Reconstructing it would have cost a lot of money so they abandoned work on the beach and devised a new plan.

Although the workmen had only been able to uncover a portion of the drainage system, they had a rough idea where the drains converged and where the flood tunnel began its route to the Money Pit. Therefore, they decided to sink a shaft a short distance inland with the hope of intersecting and plugging the tunnel.

A point was selected and a shaft was sunk to a depth of 75 feet without striking seawater. Realizing that they must have missed the tunnel, the workers moved to a spot about 12 feet to the south and started another hole. They dug down 35 feet and struck a large boulder. On prying it up they immediately encountered a rush of water. Within minutes the shaft was filled to tide level, which proved that they had struck the tunnel. They then drove heavy wood stakes into the bottom of the shaft and partially filled it with clay soil.

Having attempted to block the flood tunnel with the wood stakes, the search crew returned to the task of trying to bail out the Money Pit. This time they were able to lower the water slightly with the pumping gins but not enough to be of any value.

Desperation must have set in at this point for they repeated the same procedure that had failed them earlier that year and had failed the Onslow Company in 1804. They again tried to reach the bottom of the Money Pit by lateral tunneling. This time they dug a shaft slightly south of their first one on the same side of the Money Pit to a depth of 112 feet. As with their first shaft, no water was encountered until they almost reached the bottom of the Pit. Then, again, they were driven out when water burst into the tunnel and flooded the shaft.

The following year (1851) they tried to raise additional funds to

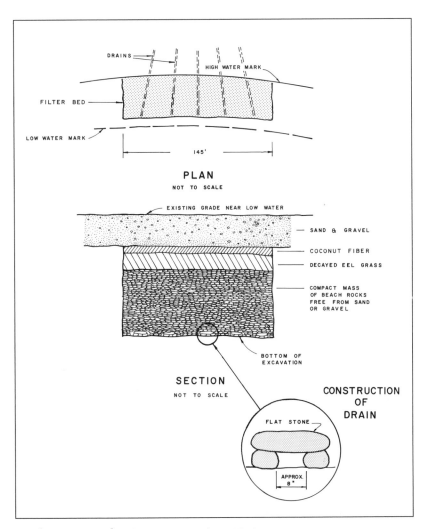

Findings at Smith's Cove excavation, 1850.

continue the search but the failure of the previous year discouraged investors and the Truro Company's operation ceased, even though most of its members had learned enough to be convinced that a vast treasure lay buried far beneath the Island's surface.

To investors, the Truro Company's undertaking had been a colossal flop, since a lot of money had been spent without recovering a single coin of treasure. But their work was not without worth for they had set in place a large piece of the Oak Island puzzle. As a result of their efforts, it would later be confirmed that the beach had been reconstructed to serve as a giant filter to furnish a constant supply of water to the bottom of the Money Pit as the tides ebbed and flowed.

SIX

Captain Kidd and Other Suspects

Captain William Kidd has long been credited with the works found on Oak Island. The early searchers believed that Kidd deposited an enormous treasure on the Island and old accounts refer to "Kidd's Treasure." The belief that Kidd was the genius behind the stupendous project is popular and is said to have originated with the early settlers from New England. But, was Kidd really the one responsible? Many investigators of the Oak Island mystery discredit the Kidd theory; furthermore, most historians agree that he was not a pirate.

Details of Kidd's childhood and youth are obscure but he was probably born in Greenock, Scotland, in 1645. His year of birth is derived from a statement made by the Newgate prison chaplain, Paul Lorrain in 1701 who reported him "about 56 years of age."

Kidd is said to have spent most of his life at sea, beginning in his boyhood days, and to have been a crew member of the *Prince Royal* during the Dutch wars, having been pressed into the navy in 1673.

By 1680, at the age of 35, Kidd had apparently prospered well from his seafaring life for he resigned from the navy and bought his own ship. Eight years later he settled in New York, bought a house and began courting Mrs. Sarah Oort, the wife of a shipmaster-merchant. Illiterate but lovely and accomplished, Sarah had first married Alderman William Cox when she was 15. He died three years later.

Kidd's courtship with Sarah was cut short in 1689 when war broke out between England and France and he was placed in command of a privateer.

The laws of that era permitted the captain of a private ship to capture ships of the enemy. The share Kidd could obtain from the spoils through privateering far exceeded what he might have hoped to earn by trading up and down the New England coast. He was probably eager to accept the commission.

Sailing to the West Indies, Kidd captured a French ship and sold it to Colonel Hewitson of New York who renamed her *Blessed William* in honor of the reigning King William III. Hewitson turned her over to Kidd's command. Following this success Kidd fell into battle with six French privateers off the coast of Antigua and captured two.

In February 1690, Kidd dropped anchor in Antigua for ship repairs and to take on fresh water and supplies. While ashore, the crew of the *Blessed William* mutinied under the leadership of Robert Culliford and set sail for New York following the capture of two Spanish ships and a raid on the island of Blanquilla.

Governor Codrington of Antigua felt compassion for Kidd's misfortune. He ruled that Kidd had given his crew no reason to mutiny and gave Kidd command of a recently captured French ship, renamed the *Antigua*. Having learned of the *Blessed William*'s destination, Kidd sat off in hot pursuit but never caught up.

The *Blessed William* arrived in New York in May 1690 for a refit and sale of her cargo. Then her crew set sail for the Gulf of Saint Lawrence where they captured six prizes. They then returned to New York and sold the *Blessed William* and transferred to one of their prizes which they had renamed the *Jacob*. Kidd just missed them when he arrived in New York in March 1691.

Kidd decided to remain in New York for awhile apparently because of Sarah Oort. Sarah's husband died on May 5, 1691, and Kidd wasn't long in taking his place. Kidd and Sarah took out a marriage license just 11 days following Mr. Oort's demise.

Kidd is said to have substantially increased his net worth by marrying Sarah. Her real estate holdings were extensive and Kidd obtained what is now the most expensive property in the world. His holdings included 56 Wall Street, 86-90 and 119-21 Pearl Street, 52-56 Water Street and 25, 27 and 29 Pine Street, in downtown New York.

The Kidds were prominent residents of New York. In the prestigious Episcopal Church on Wall Street, they held pew number 16. Sarah bore them two children over the years. The first was a girl who died in infancy and the second was a son who died, probably in his late teens or early twenties, for the year of his death was 1715.

Despite his substantial wealth increased by his marriage to Sarah, Kidd continued his privateering career and in 1691 he captured a French ship for which he was awarded 150 pounds by the Governor and Council of New York. But Kidd apparently overstepped his privileges as a privateer when he sailed into a fleet of British and colonial ships and commandeered supplies. This act probably bordered on piracy for although Kidd maintained that he had the right under his privateer's commission to commandeer supplies, he was reprimanded without punishment and lost his privateering commission.

But Kidd didn't give up his life as a man of the sea. In 1695, he was given command of the brigantine *Arigo* and delivered a cargo to London. While there Kidd met a fellow New Yorker, Robert Livingston, who had arrived in England to testify at a Board of Trade Inquiry regarding irregularities involving Benjamin Fletcher, Governor of New York, as Fletcher had blocked payments for office positions that Livingston held. Kidd and his young brother-in-law, Samuel Bradley, were persuaded by Livingston to appear as witnesses before the Board and on August 28, 1695, Kidd testified that Fletcher had rigged a recent provincial election by bringing illegal voters off the ships. Subsequently, in 1695, as a result of the inquiry, King William replaced Fletcher with Richard Coote, Earle of Bellomont, as governor of New York.

Being a man of age 50 and of considerable financial and social stature, Kidd probably would have obtained command of a royal frigate and remained in his comfortable circumstance for the balance of his life had it not been for the pirate menace of the day and his friend Livingston.

The East Indian Company wanted positive action against piracy and the British government wanted to respond to the company's wishes.

Also, King William III wanted to enrich the country with a portion of the pirate prizes.

Bellomont organized an antipiracy expedition backed by four of England's most prominent men and he informed Livingston of the undertaking. All that was now needed was an able leader and Livingston highly recommended Kidd. Kidd was at first reluctant to accept the command but finally gave in to persistent persuasion that appealed to his sense of loyalty.

To conduct the antipiracy expedition, Kidd was given a new ship of 287 tons with 34 guns. Christened the *Adventure Galley*, she set sail from Deptford on February 27, 1696, with a crew of 70 men.

Bad luck plagued Kidd from the beginning. At Nore in the estuary of the Thames, a press gang of the H.M.S. *Dutchess of Queensborough* took 20 of his best men. The regulations of the time allowed men to be pressed into naval and military duty, even if they were recruited on another ship. Kidd complained to Lord Admiral Russell at Sittingbourne and 20 men were returned—but they were not the same men.

Enraged by the exchange of crew, Kidd set sail from Plymouth on April 23, 1696, for New York. Crossing the Atlantic, Kidd captured a French banker (a boat engaged in cod fishing on the Newfoundland banks) en route for Newfoundland and had it condemned in New York for 350 pounds.

In New York, he recruited an additional 85 men of dubious character and probably worse than his existing crew as many were wharf rats and pirates—undisciplined and greedy for the rewards of plunder.

Finally, with his unsavory crew aboard, Kidd set sail for the Indian Ocean on September 6, 1696, and rounded the Cape of Good Hope in December. After going ashore for provisions and water, Kidd then headed west up the Mozambique Channel and reached the Comora Islands in February 1697. Believing that all the pirates were at sea, Kidd set off for the East coast of Africa in search of a prize but the expedition proved fruitless and the *Adventure* returned to the Comora Islands in the early summer of 1697 for scraping and caulking.

While in the Islands, tragedy struck in the form of cholera and scurvy. Kidd lost 50 of his crew in a week. Desperate for replacements, Kidd picked up 30 men off one of the beaches. These men were more raffish and malingering than the ones who had died, thus increasing the cutthroat content of his crew.

Fearing mutiny by a grossly unsatisfied crew, hungry for plunder, and also fearing that he might not be able to provide a return on the antipiracy expedition, Kidd attacked a lagging Moorish ship of a 14-ship convoy off the African Coast. But he abandoned the assault when it appeared that he might not succeed and headed for the Malabar coast of India where he hoped to finally capture pirate ships and pacify his roguish crew.

Off the West Indian coast, Kidd attacked the Moorish ship *Mary* which was commanded by an Englishman named Parker. Kidd's men lifted coffee, pepper, and twenty pieces of gold from the *Mary* and then flogged some of her men in an attempt to make them disclose if the ship carried additional hidden valuables. Finding no more loot, the *Mary* was cut free but Captain Parker was taken hostage to serve as a pilot due to his knowledge of the Malabar Coast.

With rumblings of mutiny increasing, Kidd apprehensively cruised up the Malabar Coast hoping desperately to encounter a pirate ship. It was during this excursion that Kidd committed an act that sealed his fate. He scolded William Moore, the ship's gunner, for mumbling to himself about a failure to attack a passing Dutch ship. A quarrel ensued between the two and in the heat of the argument Kidd struck the gunner with a wooden bucket inflicting a mortal wound. The gunner died the following day.

Following William Moore's death, the *Adventure* continued up the Coast and in November the Dutch ship *Rouparelle* was spotted. Kidd captured the *Rouparelle* and was delighted by the discovery that she was a French charter vessel, making the capture legal under his privateer's commission. But she wasn't much of a prize. Her cargo consisted of baled cotton, some quilts, sugar, and two horses. Nevertheless, Kidd took his captured ship in tow and renamed her *November*.

Now Kidd's luck seemed to have finally turned for on January 30, 1698, he captured the 400 ton Indian vessel *Quedah Merchant* carrying a rich cargo of silks, muslins, gold, jewels, sugar, iron, saltpeter, and guns. Her cargo has been estimated to have been worth between 40,000 and 70,000 pounds. Like his previous capture of the *Rouparelle*, the *Quedah* was also sailing under the authority of a French pass, making its capture legal. Kidd divided up the booty keeping one-quarter for himself and the sponsors, set the *Quedah*'s crew ashore, and headed for

St. Mary's Island off the Madagascar Coast with the *November* and *Quedah* now members of his fleet.

Kidd arrived at St. Mary's Island on April 1, 1698, and found the *Mocha*, a stolen East Indian frigate at anchor. To Kidd's surprise, she was commanded by his old foe Robert Culliford who had seized the *Blessed William* in Antiqua in 1690. Kidd ordered an attack on the *Mocha* and a skirmish followed in which 97 of his crew deserted to Culliford and then plundered and burned the *November*. The *Mocha* then sailed away leaving Kidd with a skeleton crew to complete his mission. As the *Adventure* was leaking badly, Kidd stripped her of anything useful and burned the hull for its iron.

Kidd was now anxious to return home but the southwest monsoons blow in the Indian Ocean from April to October so Kidd had no alternative but to sit and wait for the northwest trade winds in November.

While Kidd waited for the winds, the East Indian Company made its complaints to the British Board of Trade regarding Indian Ocean piracies. In a sheath of reports laid before the board, Kidd's name was badly blackened. Subsequently, the British government decided to put an end to piracy by issuing an amnesty and on December 8, 1698, a pardon was proclaimed to all pirates who would turn themselves in before April 30, 1699. The amnesty excluded Kidd and Captain John Avery (Long Ben) who was one of the most feared pirates of his day.

Kidd set sail for home on November 15, 1698, and as he worked his way around the Cape a net was strung out to apprehend him. On November 23, colonial governors from Massachusetts to Jamaica were ordered to seize Kidd on sight.

When Kidd arrived in the Leeward Islands in April 1699, he learned that he had been denounced as a pirate and that orders for his arrest had been issued. If Kidd was to make it home without being captured he would have to ditch the *Quedah* in favor of a fast anonymous ship.

At Mona Passage, Kidd purchased the sloop *Antonia* from a merchant by the name of Henry Bolton, transferred a portion of the *Quedah*'s booty to the *Antonia*, moored the *Quedah* up a remote river in Hispaniola, and set sail for New York.

Kidd arrived in Long Island Sound in early June 1699 and waited offshore while his lawyer, James Emmott, tried to make arrangements with the Governor of New York, Lord Bellomont, to have the warrant for arrest rescinded. Emmott gave the Governor French passes from the

November and *Quedah* to prove Kidd's innocence. The Governor responded by writing a message to Kidd that a pardon could only be granted if he could provide satisfactory proof to refute the great variety of charges.

On receiving the letter, Kidd re-evaluated his position and decided to cache a portion of his booty as a bargaining tool. He buried a major load of gold and jewels in an orchard on Gardener's Island near the eastern end of Long Island Sound, with the permission of the island's owner, John Gardner. Gardner received some gifts and gave Kidd a receipt for the buried treasure.

Following his business on Gardener's Island, Kidd arrived in Boston to appear before Bellomont and the Executive Council, confident that the two French passes would gain him a pardon. Then, while in Boston, Bellomont ordered his arrest and he was bound in irons and thrown into Stone Prison on July 6, 1699.

The sponsors could only save themselves by making Kidd a scapegoat; the passes from the *Quedah* and the *Rouparelle* were disposed of. Now Kidd had no defense.

Captain Kidd being tried for piracy; 1700 drawing.

While Kidd was in prison, Bellomont had the cache on Gardener's Island and the *Antonia* confiscated. The treasure was officially valued at 14,000 pounds.

After spending over a year in Stone Prison, Kidd was sent home in February 1700 in the warship *Advice* to stand trial before the Admiralty Court.

Kidd was tried at Old Bailey and found guilty of piracy and the murder of his gunner, William Moore. The trial is said to have been "most irregular."

Captain William Kidd was hanged in chains at Execution Dock, Wapping, on May 23, 1701.

From the overview of Kidd's life, it is apparent that those who think he was responsible for the Oak Island works are deluding themselves. Kidd lacked the time and the manpower to carry out the project. Also, the bulk of his treasure has been accounted for.

Kidd commanded an unruly crew. It is inconceivable that such an undisciplined lot could be forced into the manual labor that must have been expended on such a large undertaking. Also, the designer and builder of the complex system found on Oak Island was a highly skilled and ingenious engineer. Although Kidd was a capable seaman, he was not known to possess any appreciable engineering skills.

Engineers have estimated that it took an army of men two years to carry out the mysterious excavations. Kidd's voyages simply do not provide sufficient time gaps, either on his five-month voyage from St. Mary's Island, Madagascar, to the Leeward Islands or on his three-month jaunt from Hispaniola to New York Sound. Kidd did not have the time to visit Nova Scotia and construct the Oak Island complex.

The quantity of treasure remaining after sharing with his crew could not have bankrolled the Oak Island undertaking. Kidd shared three-quarters of the booty with his men. Applying the liberal estimate of 70,000 pounds as the value of the *Quedah* cache, 17,500 pounds remained. Kidd then dipped into the balance to purchase the *Antonia* from Henry Bolton. The tally of booty remaining on Gardener's Island and the *Antonia* was 14,000 pounds. So, there would have been little if any treasure remaining to bury on Oak Island.

However, despite the facts, the name Captain Kidd has become a synonymous for pirate and it has been directly associated with Oak Island. Perhaps only after a treasure is unearthed and the true identity of its depositor known, will Kidd be released from the general belief that he was responsible for the Island's labyrinth of pits, vaults, and tunnels.

Aside from Kidd, some of the most favored names associated with Oak Island include Blackbeard (Edward Teach) (unknown–1718), William Dampier (1652–1715), Henry Morgan (1635–1688), and William Phipps (1651–1695).

Of these four very well known men of opportunity only Phipps can be taken seriously. The others did their plundering mostly in southern waters, preying on richly laden Spanish galleons in the West Indies. They would have had no incentive to sail 2,000 miles north to Nova Scotia to bury their caches. There were hundreds of coral beach islands available to them on which they could easily dig a hole and stockpile booty.

Phipps was born in Pemmaquid (Bristol), Maine, in 1651 and started his early working days as a ship's carpenter. Continuing his marine life, he took to the sea in the 1680s as a privateer in his own ship and in 1687 recovered a 30 ton Spanish treasure ship wrecked on a shoal off the coast of Hispaniola. He took his prize to England, shared it with the Crown, and was accordingly knighted and made the High Sheriff of New England. In May 1690, as a privateer, he set out with seven ships and 700 men on an attack against Port Royal on the Bay of Fundy shore of Nova Scotia where his men pillaged and plundered the little French settlement. Menneval, the French Commander, had only 86 men and weak fortifications. Needless to say, the French were no match for Phipps with his overpowering forces. Continuing his raid, Phipps turned back towards Maine, rounded the southwestern end of Nova Scotia, sailed up the coast, and plundered and burned LaHave, 25 miles from Oak Island. As further reward for his contributions to the British government he was made the first governor of Massachusetts in 1692. Phipps enjoyed the high post for a relatively short time.

It is doubtful that Phipps took the time and effort to engineer and build the Oak Island labyrinth, if indeed he had the engineering capability, in view of his death in 1695.

Rather than credit a single pirate or privateer, some modern investigators of the Oak Island mystery contend that the Money Pit is the product of a consortium. They believe that several pirates pooled their resources to construct a communal treasure bank.

Captain Teach, known as Black Beard; 1736 illustration.

William Phipps, privateer.

According to their theory, a shaft (the Money Pit) was sunken to a depth of below 100 feet and incline tunnels were driven from its bottom to large water-tight vaults situated at various locations such as the center of the Island, the mainland, and nearby Frog Island. These vaults were constructed at the ends of the tunnels just a little above sea level. Above the vaults, the virgin forest floor with trees, moss, rocks, ferns, and bushes gave no indication as to what lay below. The position of a vault was pin-pointed from measurements and bearings determined from below and referenced on the ground surface. To dig up his treasure, the pirate needed only a surface landmark, a bearing, and a distance. These values were memorized or recorded, the former being the most probable.

After completing the vaults and depositing the treasures, the pirates backfilled the Money Pit shaft and constructed the tidal flood trap. Anyone who might try to reach the bottom of the Money Pit and the entrance to the tunnels to the vaults would be flooded out.

The Money Pit's booby trap is analogous to placing a fingertip over the end of a soda straw and vertically immersing the open end into a glass of water. The column of air in the straw between the top and bottom is blocked. No water rises in the straw until the finger tip is removed and the air lock is broken.

The engineering aspect of the concept is sound and the flooding system was in fact constructed, but it is difficult to believe that pirates could have banded together to hide their caches, given the mistrust they had for one another. And, if they had, surely rumors of the operation would have eventually leaked out and surfaced in legend or recorded history.

At this point, the obvious question is whether pirates could have been involved in such an elaborate project. I think the answer is: Against the slimmest doubt, no!

All documented accounts of buried pirate treasure are of small caches buried only a few feet underground. Pirates were a lazy lot by nature. It is difficult to accept that plunder-driven scoundrels, undisciplined and having a "live for today philosophy," took the time and exerted the energy necessary to create the Oak Island complex.

So, if pirates were not responsible, who was? Perhaps the answer lies in other pieces of the puzzle.

SEVEN

The Bottom Falls Out of the Money Pit

Following the Truro Company's failure in 1849 and 1850, eleven years passed before another search was organized. Meanwhile, in 1853, a few years before his death, John Smith conveyed his property to his two sons, Joseph and Thomas. Four years later, the sons conveyed the property to Henry Stevens who a short time later conveyed it to Anthony Graves. Graves had previously acquired several other lots making him the largest land owner of the Island.

Unlike John Smith who had built near the Money Pit, Anthony Graves constructed his house and several barns at Joudrey's Cove on the north side of the Island about 1,500 feet from the old stand. Outwardly, it appears that Graves had little interest in the Money Pit but he may have been a man far ahead of his time. He is the first person to have left a hint that there is more to the mystery than the labyrinth of pits and tunnels at the Island's eastern end. It is said that Graves frequently used Spanish money when purchasing household supplies in the town of Mahone Bay, ten miles south of the Island and, in 1930, a

Spanish coin similar to the one found in 1965 on Oak Island.

silver Spanish coin, dated 1785, was found beside an old road running from his house to the shore. In 1965 a party of students from Phillips Academy, Andover, Massachusetts, discovered a Spanish coin at the site of Graves' house while conducting a survey of the Island with metal detectors. The coin was dated 1598. In the 1970s Fred Nolan displayed a collection of Spanish coins called "Pillar Dollars" (named after the Pillars of Hercules), in a museum situated on Crandall's Point. The display was loaned to him by Joseph Carsley, deceased, of Mahone Bay. Carsley, in turn, had acquired the coins from the heirs of Anthony Graves!

Despite the Truro Company's failure to raise additional funds, the zeal to bring up the casks from the bottom of the Money Pit was rekindled in 1850 by the discovery of the elaborate flood trap. News of the mysterious artificial beach and tidal flood tunnel spread like wildfire. Only something of enormous value could justify such a large expenditure of labor and time.

People previously involved in the 1849–1850 search wanted to try again and others clamored to become involved. So, on April 3, 1861, the Oak Island Association of Truro, Nova Scotia, was formed. The new consortium was headed by Samuel Retti, president, accompanied by Jotham McCully, corporate secretary, who had been with the Truro Company (1849–1850), James McNutt, secretary-treasurer who kept a diary of the operation, and George Mitchell, superintendent of works.

Besides Jotham McCully, the consortium included others who had worked on the previous operation, including Adams A. Tupper and Jefferson W. MacDonald.

The new syndicate approached Anthony Graves for permission to dig and they struck a bargain by which Graves would receive one-third of any treasure recovered.

The Oak Island Association's management was convinced that they would be able to drain the Money Pit and bring up the "treasure" with a sufficiently large work force. With that in mind, the syndicate issued 100 shares at $20 each. The objective of this substantial share offering was to obtain a large number of workmen by providing an attractive wage—$18 dollars per month, plus lodging and traveling expenses.

Eager to turn a fast buck, investors quickly snapped up the shares and the newly formed company took over where the Truro Company had left off in 1850. With a large work force consisting of 63 men and 33 horses, success seemed certain. It would simply be a matter of cutting off the water from the ocean and draining the old Pit. The cataclysm that was to follow would not only shock them, but would later suggest that the Money Pit was far more complicated than they had previously imagined.

The Money Pit had caved in over the past decade and the first item of work was to clean it out. The pit was reopened and recribbed to a depth of 88 feet at which point the crew stopped digging since the clay soil below appeared to be blocking any serious water intrusion from the yet to be located water tunnel. They decided to "leave well enough alone" so as not to repeat previous incidents of major flooding.

With the Money Pit stabilized, Superintendent Mitchell decided to make a direct attack on the flood tunnel and block it off. This would end the water problem—or so he thought. Presuming that the flood tunnel ran straight to where the drains at the shore converged, he selected a point 25 feet east of the Money Pit. The workmen excavated a shaft to a depth of 120 feet without encountering a drop of water. They had missed the water channel.

Fred Nolan and I once discussed the Oak Island Association's failure to locate the flood tunnel by digging a shaft near the Money Pit. "The clay down in that area is unbelievable," Nolan explained. "It's almost as hard as brick. The people who dug the flood tunnel must have experienced a terrible hardship." In fact, the flood tunnel does *not* follow a straight line between the Money Pit and the point on the shore where the drains running downward from low tide converge. Nolan and I concluded that the channel was crooked because the original diggers must have followed the line of least resistance. If they hit a seam of sand or a pocket of less dense soil, they took advantage of it. If they struck a granite boulder, they dug around it. So it would have been a measure of good luck rather than design if anyone had struck the flood tunnel on the first attempt.

Failing to intercept the subterranean channel, Mitchell resorted to the same scheme that had failed previously. He tried to reach the treasure vault from below by lateral tunneling. First, his crew sank a second shaft 18 feet west of the Money Pit to a depth of 118 feet. They then drove a tunnel four feet high by three feet wide for a distance of seventeen feet towards the Pit before water rushed into the tunnel. They set up a horse-powered pumping gin over the 118-foot deep shaft in an effort to control the water, but it was useless. They stopped after three days of continuous bailing, to find water seeping up through the bottom of the Money Pit.

When Mitchell then tried to reach the supposed treasure vaults from his first 120-foot deep shaft, that too failed as it began to fill with water.

Feeling the seeds of defeat setting in, Superintendent Mitchell and his men made a desperate attempt to stem the rising water. They rigged four large 70 gallon bailing casks over the Money Pit and the other two shafts, and 63 men along with 33 horses worked in shifts for a couple of days. This operation progressed rather well and almost succeeded in draining the pits but it was hampered when the tunnel connecting the 118-foot deep shaft choked up with soft clay causing the infernal water to rise once again in the Money Pit.

Two men were sent down to clear the mud from the connecting tunnel. Just half-way through the tunnel, they were stunned by a thunderous crash from above. A wall of mud pitched forward with enormous momentum. Terrified, the men ran for their lives and barely escaped being entombed. In less than three minutes, the shaft was filled with seven feet of mud.

Plank by plank, the Money Pit cribbing fell downward. It was as if the bottom had fallen out of the Pit and all the construction directly above had been swallowed up by the depths below. Samuel C. Fraser, a member of the Oak Island Association, recalled the catastrophe in a 1895 letter to A.S. Lowden, then manager of a search syndicate: "I was sent down to clean out the Money Pit, but before going into it I examined the 118-foot pit and tunnel, which was then nearly finished. At the end of the tunnel I saw every sign of the cataclysm that was about to take place and I refused to go into the Money Pit…. When the pit fell down I was there…. There went down 10,000 feet of lumber, board measure, the cribbing of the old Money Pit." The water down in the Pit was described as "boiling like a volcano." The Money Pit had collapsed and lay in ruins.

Early accounts tell us that the men recovered a couple of artifacts as they were driven from the tunnel during the collapse. They found a stick of oak timber three and a half feet in length which had been ejected by the mud, along with the bottom of a small yellow painted barrel or dish the size of a nail keg. The oak stick was described in a newspaper article in September of that year by "the digger Patric" as "stained black with age; it was cut, hewn, champered, sawn or bored, according to the purpose for which it was needed." James McNutt, writing in his diary, mentions "a piece of juniper with the bark on (and) cut at each end with an edge tool" and "a spruce slab with a mining auger hole in it."

The Oak Island Association undoubtedly received enormous flak from its backers after the cataclysm. A recent book on the Oak Island story suggests that the syndicate had "inadvertently caused the collapse" and a short story published in 1930 accuses Mitchell and his crew of "disturbing the treasure" by the tunneling process. It is easy to imagine the investors' scathing comments! They probably called the Association's directors feeble-minded fools, and branded George Mitchell a blundering idiot. But, was Mitchell and his consortium totally to blame?

Tunneling, in an attempt to reach the suspected treasure, had become a normal routine, dating back to the Lynds group in 1803. By the time Mitchell tunneled from the 118-foot shaft, the supposed bottom of the Money Pit had already been disturbed by three previous tunnels of earlier search parties. Either through technical illiteracy or blinded by obsession, both the Lynds party and the Truro Company of a half century later made the unforgivable error of trying to reach the supposed treasure hoard at the bottom of the Money Pit by tunneling from adjacent shafts. The weight of 60 feet of water in the Pit was in the magnitude of 300,000 pounds or 150 tons, but the diggers apparently gave no thought to this enormous weight that lay above as they tunneled for their treasure. The flooding was inevitable.

The Oak Island Association had almost succeeded in draining the Money Pit. It is conceivable that they would have recovered the Oak Island treasure had the ground below not been severely disturbed by the previous ventures.

EIGHT

Searching for Lost Casks

Despite the collapse of the Money Pit, the Oak Island Association persevered. Somehow, Mitchell and his partners convinced the existing backers to reinvest, or they attracted additional investors. They were able to raise an additional $2,000 and work was continued.

It was now more evident than ever before that the water entering the Money Pit had to be completely stopped either by bailing or by locating and blocking off the flood tunnel. The Association's first choice was to bail.

Since the steam engine had become the modern means of accomplishing heavy and labor-intensive tasks, Superintendent Mitchell decided to abandon the use of horses and had the necessary equipment barged over to the Island.

In the fall of the year the Money Pit collapsed (1861), they set up pumps driven by steam engines but the operation had just gotten underway when tragedy struck. In 1868, E.H. Owen of Lunenburg wrote this account of the first death in the Oak Island Saga:

"The boiler of one company burst, whereby one man was scalded to death and others injured. The water was pumped out by a large barrel-shaped tube, made of thin materials, and reaching to some distance into the Pit. The stream of water was conducted from this into the sea by means of a long wooden trough which extended down to the shore." Work was halted for the winter. The Oak Island mystery had claimed its first victim; others would follow.

The Oak Island Association presumed that the platforms and casks that had been drilled through between 98 and 105 feet in 1849 had slid into the tunnel from the 118-foot west shaft during the collapse of the Money Pit. Measurements showed the excavated bottom had dropped from 88 feet to about 102 feet, or 14 feet, suggesting that the lower platform that the casks rested on was now at about the 119-foot level. This presumption was supported by the artifacts recovered by the men who escaped the rush of mud when the Pit collapsed. Their plan was to recover the casks by tunnelling from the bottom of the collapsed Pit, but first the water problem would have to be solved.

Although the first attempt to apply steam power ended in disaster, the Association was determined to try it again. They were sure that technology would triumph over obsolete methods. So, with a winter of rest behind them, Mitchell and his men returned the following spring with renewed energy and enthusiasm. And, they also had a new plan to use a steam-driven pump. They would excavate a pumping shaft adjacent and connected to the Money Pit and pump the Pit dry, keeping it dry while they cleared it out and recovered the treasure.

Accordingly, they sank a shaft to a depth of 107 feet and put a steam-driven pump into action. This new approach worked well for a while, and the Money Pit was cleaned out and recribbed to a depth of 103 feet, where water began seeping up through the bottom of the Pit and exceeded the capacity of the pump.

Money was running out. It was time to initiate something fast and efficient.

Mitchell and his men quickly gathered up their tools and equipment and tried another tack at Smith's Cove. They picked a point a short distance inland from the shore and began digging a new shaft, expecting to strike the elusive water tunnel. They worked late into the evenings and dug to a depth of 50 feet before admitting defeat. They had missed the tunnel!

Pressed to find the water channel, they began digging tunnels out from the bottom of the shaft in various directions—to no avail. They concluded that they were digging from too low a depth and moved up to a higher level. They dug more tunnels, without results. In desperation, Mitchell continued to dig for the water tunnel from two more levels—without luck.

Where was the flood tunnel?

Frustrated but still determined, Mitchell ordered his men to the beach of Smith's Cove in order to plug the drainage system. They couldn't build a cofferdam due to lack of funds, so their work was confined to an area close to the shore.

The men uncovered and removed 30 to 40 feet of the box drains and packed them full with clay. Although this halved the flow of water to the Money Pit, it proved to be temporary. The tides quickly washed out the clay. The only beneficial outcome of all this work was to finally prove the existence of a water channel. Clogging the drains caused the water in the Money Pit to become muddy.

Now, Mitchell was at his wit's end, without a clue as to how to proceed. So he began to "flog a dead horse."

Moving back to the Money Pit, he had a shaft dug about 100 feet southeast of the Pit and drove a tunnel towards Smith's Cove in hopes of intercepting the drainage system and diverting the water to this shaft. It was no use.

At this point, one might have expected the Oak Island Association to give up, but they drove on.

Next, Mitchell and his men drove a tunnel from this latest shaft towards the Money Pit, still trying to divert the water. They struck the Pit at the 108-foot depth, slightly above the water level that was being maintained by pumps on connecting shafts.

They cribbed the Money Pit down an additional five feet to the 108-foot level and tunneled out in various directions in search of the lost casks. They continued this laborious and repetitive work into the following year of 1864, without encountering a trace of the casks drilled through in 1849.

During the tunneling work of 1864, Mitchell and Company struck the flood tunnel from Smith's Cove where it entered the east side of the Money Pit at the depth of around 110 feet. Fraser wrote in his letter of 1895: "As we entered the old place of the treasure we cut off the mouth of the 'Pirate Tunnel.' As we opened it, the water hurled around rocks about twice the size of a man's head, with many smaller, and drove the men back for protection. We could not go into the shaft again, for about nine hours. Then pumps conquered and we went down and cleared it out. The tunnel was found near the top of our tunnel. I brought Mr. Hill, the engineer, down and he put his arm into the hole of the tunnel, up to his shoulder.... Nothing could be more particular than our search in the old place of the old treasure. There was no mistake about our search in the old treasure place." Fraser describes the construction of the flood tunnel as "made of round stones, such as are found abundantly on the beach and field around the Island." They further verified the existence of the tunnel by dumping cart-loads of clay onto the beach where the fan-shaped drains converged. The water in the Money Pit became muddy within a half hour.

At last they were able to verify the existence of a man-made connection between the sea and the Money Pit, but no one could figure out how to turn off the water.

Flat broke, the Oak Island Association had no alternative but to fold its operation.

Two years later, on May 3, 1866, the Oak Island Eldorado Company (also known as the Halifax Company) sprang to life. The new company raised $4,000 by selling 200 shares at $20 each. Their plan was to build a substantial wood and clay dam to encompass the entire rock drainage system of Smith's Cove, pump out all the water inside the dam, and completely cut off the flood tunnel. The prospectus assured that "There cannot be any doubt this mode of operation must succeed and will lead to the development of the hidden treasure, so long sought for."

Subsequently, the company's workmen constructed a cofferdam— 12 feet high and 375 feet long—at Smith's Cove. It extended out and encompassed the artificial beach, its drains running down from low tide to the flood tunnel. They emptied the water from the enclosed area but before the Money Pit could be pumped dry for excavation to continue, storms and unusual high tides destroyed the dam.

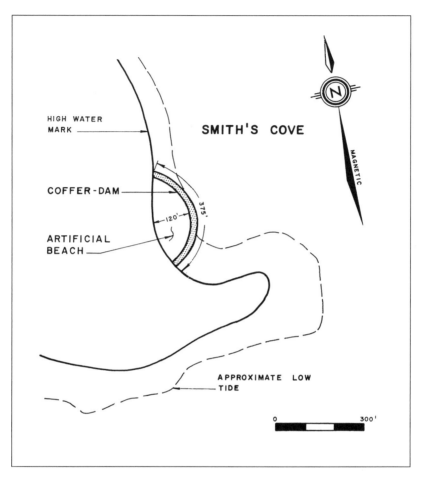

HIGH WATER
MARK

SMITH'S COVE

COFFER-DAM

375'

120'

ARTIFICIAL
BEACH

APPROXIMATE LOW
TIDE

0   300'

Plan showing approximate location of the cofferdam constructed in 1866 to stop the flow of water to the Money Pit.

The Eldorado group resorted to drilling in an attempt to locate the missing casks since they now believed that they had dropped down to a lower level (caused by the collapse of the Money Pit in 1861). The drilling operation stretched from November 26, 1866 to January 7, 1867. After setting up a platform at the 90-foot level, they struck spruce wood at 110 feet. They brought up coconut fiber, chips of wood, and charcoal from 128 feet. At 132 feet, they recovered oak borings, chips of spruce or poplar wood, and more coconut fiber. Further drilling to a depth of 158 feet brought up nothing of significance. Additional drilling from a higher location to a depth of 163 feet yielded no results. They abandoned the program.

The Oak Island Association had excavated a labyrinth of tunnels and the Eldorado Company had drilled deep holes, both in search of the casks that had gone down with the Money Pit's collapse. All, to no avail. The searchers were more baffled when they ended the search than when they began.

NINE

The Cave-In-Pit

Once the Oak Island Eldorado Company closed down their operation in 1867, 26 years passed before another serious attempt was made to match wits with the unknown genius who engineered the Money Pit.

The quest to unravel the mystery might have remained dormant for a very long time had it not been for a dramatic incident that occurred 12 years after the Eldorado group abandoned the search.

One day in the spring of 1878, Sophia Sellers, daughter of Anthony Graves, was plowing the farm field about 350 feet east of the Money Pit with a team of oxen when suddenly the ground in front of her collapsed. The plow handles were ripped from her hands and with a sickening crash, the plow and oxen disappeared. Kicking and thrashing, the beasts dropped into a hole as deep as a single-storey house is high. Snorting and kicking, the trapped animals fought to free themselves from a likely grave. Sophia ran for help and returned with her husband along with some recruited help. They looped ropes and straps around the trapped animals and harnessed them to teams of oxen and horses. Tediously, the exhausted oxen were hauled to the surface and cut free from a tangled mess of rigging.

The hole, later dubbed the Cave-in-Pit, was fifteen to eighteen feet deep and six to eight feet across. It was situated directly over the supposed line of the flood tunnel.

Because the Cave-in-Pit was presumed to be directly over the course of the water channel, many concluded that it was related to the original Money Pit project. Speculation ran high as to what it represented. Experienced miners believed that the Cave-in-Pit was an air hole that was sunk in order to ventilate the 500-foot long tunnel. Others conjectured that the Cave-in-Pit held the key to shutting off the water by means of a gate or valve. Still others suggested that a secret tunnel ran from the bottom of the hole to a treasure vault.

Interest peaked in 1885 when a boatswain's whistle was found on the Island in the soil below high tide at Smith's Cove. It was of an ancient and peculiar design and made of bone or ivory. A few years later, a young man spotted a copper coin on the Island. It was dated 1317. It weighed an ounce and a half and is said to have borne strange marks. (According to some versions of this discovery, the coin's date was 1713—perhaps to better fit into the pirate era, when the Money Pit works were believed to have been carried out.)

Sophia Sellers and her husband seem to have shared Graves' disinterest in the Money Pit because they back-filled the Cave-in-Pit with rocks, resurfaced the gap in the field with top soil, and continued cultivating the eastern end of the Island as if nothing had happened. Unlike the original discoverers of the Money Pit, the Sellers didn't seek a backer to pursue this new discovery. It would be picked up later, by someone outside the family. The man who was to carry on the legacy was Frederick Leander Blair. At the time of the discovery of the Cave-in-Pit, he was an 11-year-old living in Amherst, Nova Scotia.

As a boy, Blair used to hear about the Oak Island story from his Uncle Isaac Blair and Jefferson W. MacDonald who had both worked on the Island in the 1860s. They told him many pertinent facts about the original works and the early expeditions.

Confident that he could solve the mystery, at the age of 26, Blair formed the Oak Island Treasure Company in 1893. Its head office was at Kittery in the State of Maine. Blair had been working as an insurance salesman in Boston and thanks to his good salesmanship, he was able to attract the key people he needed to establish the firm.

Anthony Graves, who owned most of the Island including the east end where the Money Pit is situated, died in 1887. He left his property to his daughters: Sophia, wife of Henry Sellers of Chester Basin, and Rachel, wife of Abraham Ernst of the town of Mahone Bay. Blair approached the Sellers and Ernst families and struck a deal. The new company would lease the land for three years for $30,000 and the rights to 100 percent of everything recovered. The price was a large sum of money in those days, and it showed Blair's faith in the venture.

The new company was incorporated under the laws of the State of Maine with A.M. Bridgman of Brockton, Massachusetts, as president; H.C. Tupper was treasurer; and George E. Houghton of Roxbury and C.C.L. Moore of Malden were directors. The company had authorized capital of $60,000 in shares of $5 each. With $30,000 set aside to cover the three-year lease, the Company hoped to carry out the work from the proceeds of the sale of just 1,000 shares, and then divide the remaining unsold stock pro rata among the stockholders at the end of the project.

It can be assumed that Blair was targeting American investors from his U.S. headquarters, and it is interesting to note that the bulk of the shares were purchased by Nova Scotians. Others included Bostonians and residents from elsewhere in New England.

Blair was a diligent researcher. He interviewed people who had previously worked on the Island including Jotham B. McCully, Robert Creelman, and mining engineer Adams A. Tupper, all of whom worked from 1849 to 1850 and in later explorations. Creelman passed on accounts of the 1795 and 1803 work that he had learned from two of the original discoverers, John Smith and Anthony Vaughan. Blair also interviewed Sophia Sellers, John McGinnis, Arthur McGinnis, and George Vaughan. The last three were direct descendents of two of the original discoverers, Daniel McGinnis and Anthony Vaughan.

After compiling a wealth of information, Blair and Adams A. Tupper prepared the company's prospectus which briefly told the Oak Island story. It stated:

"Much fiction has been written concerning great sums of money and vast quantities of jewels buried by pirates some 200 years ago somewhere along the Atlantic coast. Our story has to do only with facts, as stated by the men now living and who had a hand in them, or as told to them by men now dead. It can be proven:

1. That a shaft about 13 feet in diameter and 100 feet deep was sunk on Oak Island in Mahone Bay, Nova Scotia, before the memory of any now living.
2. That the shaft was connected by an underground tunnel with the open ocean, about 365 feet distant. [This distance is more accurately about 500 feet.]
3. That at the bottom of this shaft were placed large wooden boxes in which were precious metals and jewels.
4. That many attempts have been made, without success, to obtain this treasure.
5. That it is reasonably certain the treasure is large, because so great a trouble would never have been taken to conceal any small sum.
6. That it is now entirely feasible to thoroughly explore this shaft and recover the treasure still located therein."

The prospectus went on to disclose the reported *modus operandis*: "It is perfectly evident that the great mistake thus far has been in attempting to 'bail out' the ocean through the various pits. The present company intends to use best modern appliances for cutting off the flow of water through the tunnel, at some point near the shore, before attempting to pump out the water. It believes, from investigations already made, that such an attempt will be completely successful; and if it is, there can be no trouble in pumping out the 'money pit' as dry as when the treasure was first placed there."

Work began in the summer of 1894. In accordance with the prospectus, the first objective was to shut off the flow of water in the flood tunnel, near the shore. The point selected for this first phase of the project was the Cave-in-Pit.

While removing rocks that the Sellers had used to infill the Cave-in-Pit, the workmen found themselves in a well-defined circular shaft that was obviously part of the original project. They were able to remove the soil from this shaft without the use of picks, but the sides were of very hard clay—too hard for even the picks.

They excavated the Cave-in-Pit to a depth of about 52 feet and then drilled a hole vertically from the bottom an additional 16 feet...without striking water. The next day, sea water broke into the pit, presumably from an adjacent shaft or a tunnel from an earlier search. It filled to tide level. Attempts to bail out the pit were futile; the water could not be lowered.

After failing to shut off the flow of water to the Money Pit, the Oak Island Treasure Company held a meeting on April 2, 1895, at which A.S. Lowden was appointed general manager for the summer of that year.

Lowden proposed to make another attempt to block the flow of water in the flood tunnel, and then to "attack the Money Pit direct."

Neither plan worked. The Money Pit had been filled in by the Oak Island Eldorado Company in 1867, while the other adjacent shafts had been filled in by either the diggers or Anthony Graves. Over the 26 years spanning the search, the shafts had lost their identities through erosion and vegetation.

This meant that Lowden's group was unable to ascertain which shaft was the Money Pit. The workmen reached a depth of 55 feet in what they thought was the Money Pit, but once again they were driven out by water. Further progress would have been made but the company was badly in need of a larger pump and although there was more stock to be sold, Lowden was unable to raise the necessary funds.

The Oak Island Treasure Company was in trouble. It needed more than Blair's optimism and enthusiasm to keep it going. The times called for drastic measures.

TEN

The Hidden Cement Chamber

As the Oak Island Treasure Company struggled with its lack of direction, dissension arose between Bostonians and Nova Scotians over details of operation and management. Nova Scotia shareholders demanded that operations be carried out by Nova Scotian directors—not by directors from faraway Boston. The Nova Scotians held a meeting in November 1895 and decided to send a delegation of stockholders to meet with the Boston directors. As a result, a new board of management was appointed. Under the new regime, the Nova Scotian shareholders gained control of operations. The new board consisted of T. Perley Putnam of Onslow, as manager; Frederick Blair, who was now living in Amherst, as treasurer; George W. Fullerton of Pictou; W.H. McDonald of Amherst; and William Chappell, a lumberman and manufacturer from Amherst. Captain John William Welling of Amherst was chosen as director of operations.

With the reorganization of the company, the prospectus was revised to include an "addition" which provided more information about the mystery of Oak Island. The principals initiated a vigorous stock selling campaign to raise $2,000 for a new steam pump and boiler.

In October 1896 the workmen focused once again on the Money Pit. The shaft thought to be the Money Pit which was begun the previous year was pumped dry with the new pumping equipment and then re-excavated to a depth of 70 feet where the same old story replayed itself. The water intrusion overcame the pump's capacity to handle it. Next, they cleaned out the old 75-foot deep shaft that the Truro Company had dug near Smith's Cove in 1850. They deepened it to 78 feet, at which point water rushed in from an old tunnel of the 1860s. They were able to control the water by installing a pump on this shaft, and work continued.

At about this time, the quest for Captain Kidd's would-be treasure claimed its second victim. On March 26, 1897, Maynard Kaiser of Gold River was sent down into a shaft containing water to recover a cask that had fallen to the bottom. He was told to bring up the empty cask. Instead, he filled it and tried to ride it to the surface. The extra weight overtaxed the hoisting equipment and the rope slipped off the pulley, dropping the cask back to the bottom. Kaiser was killed in the fall.

As a result of the accident, most of the workers walked off the job. One of the men is said to have dreamt that Captain Kidd appeared to warn him that he planned to kill anyone who tried to recover his treasure. It is thought that the workmen heeded the warning, but in all likelihood, the men considered the operation unsafe. The Halifax *Chronicle-Herald* ran an article in June 1894 that stated: "Two of the treasure seekers had a miraculous escape from death Friday morning. It appears that while engaged in excavating 'test pit' No. 3, [probably the Cave-in-Pit] part of the hoisting apparatus gave way, precipitating the tub to within 10 feet of the bottom of the shaft, where it struck the cribbing, upset and emptied its contents of rock and earth on the heads of the two terrified excavators in the pit. Happily, with the exception of a few slight bruises, no one was hurt."

After a temporary delay during which some of the men were persuaded back while others were replaced, the work on the presumed Money Pit was resumed. They reached a depth of 110 feet on April 22, 1897, at which point they found a tunnel built by the 1860s searchers. They entered it and a short distance inside came upon an intersecting tunnel which they followed to its end, where they found a well cribbed shaft, 9 feet square, which extended far up into the darkness. James McGinnis, a direct descendent of Daniel McGinnis (one of the original discoverers), told the searchers that the Oak Island Eldorado Company (1866–1867) had built a strong drilling platform in the Money Pit at the 30-foot level and filled in the top 30 feet before discontinuing operations. Digging down from above, they uncovered a platform at the 30-foot level and concluded that they had excavated the wrong shaft—the shaft thought to be the Money Pit which was begun in 1895—and were now in the Money Pit itself. Blair wrote: "Water was boiling up through the bottom of this pit, and it proved to be the real Money Pit."

At 111 feet down in the Money Pit the crew discovered a well-defined two and a half foot wide opening in the east wall, which they determined was the flood tunnel outlet. Sea water gushed from the opening with great force and pressure. The sides and top of the tunnel had been cut from solid clay. The sides were vertical, the top horizontal, and the hole was filled with beach stones, gravel, and sand. Several accounts give the height of the tunnel as four feet but Welling notes that the full height couldn't be ascertained due to the increasing volume of water gushing from the tunnel. A bird's bone, a chip of wood, and a piece of bark taken from the sand and gravel confirmed a connection with the sea.

The velocity and volume of water entering the Money Pit became more than the pumps could handle. Soon the Money Pit and adjacent shaft filled to tide level, bringing the operation to a standstill.

Blair and his group were facing failure as they concocted a desperate plan to shut off the flood tunnel. They would set off huge underground dynamite charges in a line of holes strung across the tunnel and destroy it, once and for all.

They drilled five holes 15 feet apart and 80 to 95 feet deep on a line about 50 feet from the high water mark of the shore of Smith's Cove, crossing the supposed line of the flood tunnel at right angles. Only the third hole—the one over the supposed tunnel—struck water. The saltwater they encountered at a depth of 80 feet rose to tide level and fluctuated with the tides. It appeared that they might have at last located the water channel that had defeated all previous parties. This was confirmed when they poured water into the drill hole. It failed to raise the water level, suggesting that they had probably struck the troublesome tunnel.

They loaded each dry hole with 50 to 75 pounds of dynamite, and

The Halifax Herald Ltd.

Smith's Cove about 1897. The large pile of logs was probably for the construction of cribbing in the shafts.

filled them with water as a primer. Other than the spectacular sight of water spouting 100 feet into the air, nothing was achieved when these charges were set off. Next, they loaded an extra large charge of 160 pounds of dynamite into the third hole over the supposed tunnel, and detonated it. This time the water didn't gush from the hole but the water in both the Money Pit and Cave-in-Pit foamed and boiled, indicating that they had pinpointed the exact position of the flood tunnel near Smith's Cove.

What surprised the searchers was the location of the tunnel—80 feet deep, and so close to shore. To explain this excessive depth, Blair and his men surmised that the water dropped through a vertical hole from the point where the fan-shaped drains converged to a catch basin about 75 feet below the beach. They theorized that a tunnel ran on a slight incline from the basin to about the 110-foot level in the Money Pit. This theory, however, was flawed because saltwater had been encountered nearby at a depth of 35 feet by a shaft in 1850, and again at 52 feet in the Cave-in-Pit in 1894. Their explanation for this inconsistency was that the third hole wasn't directly over the flood tunnel and water had broken through from the tunnel at a higher level after the 80-foot depth was reached, thus squashing the supposition that there was a 75-foot deep catch basin.

Believing that the flood tunnel was clogged as a result of the dynamite explosion, Captain Welling turned his full work-force on the Money Pit. The plan was to locate the casks lost in the 1861 collapse of the Pit which were thought to be somewhere around the 118-foot level.

With the pumps holding the water down to the 100-foot level, the crew put down several exploratory drill holes from a platform at 90 feet.

The first hole bored through five inches of well-preserved oak at the 126-foot level before striking an iron obstruction which could not be penetrated. Surprised by this encounter, Blair and Captain Welling ordered the drillers to shift a little to one side and try again.

They drilled one foot away from the first hole and this time they slipped past the obstruction at 126 feet. Continuing downward, at 153 feet 8 inches, the drill struck soft stone or cement which was seven inches thick overlaying five inches of solid oak. Below the oak was a one and a half to two inch gap followed by what William Chappell later described as "a substance the character of which no person would attempt to state." Chappell goes on to say: "After considerable twisting of the auger on the substance, it was carefully withdrawn and the borings brought up therewith were preserved by Mr. Putnam. The drill was then again put down when we found we were apparently on soft metal that could be moved slightly thereby forming a crevice or space into which the drill, when in alignment, would drop and stick and wedge."

The metal posed considerable difficulties as the crew continued to drill. They pictured metal in bars for the first four inches, followed by metal in pieces or coin as they managed to bore down through two feet eight inches where the drill struck a substance similar to the one first encountered. The drill jammed and no attempt was made to go through it. The borings that were brought up from just under 154 feet and given to Putnam consisted of oak chips, coconut fiber, and a very small mysterious artifact that still haunts people today.

Putnam personally removed and cleaned the borings from the drill. The samples were never out of his possession until they were examined by a physician, Dr. A.E. Porter, at the Court House in Amherst. The doctor studied the borings with a powerful magnifying glass in the presence of 35 or more people. Blair's lawyer, Reginald V. Harris, writes: "The strange fiber attracted his attention. Under the glass it appeared in the form of a compact ball about the size of a grain of rice, with fuzz or short hair on the surface. After working with it for some minutes he got it flattened out, when it had every appearance of being a small piece of parchment, upon which was written in black ink, characters that appeared to represent parts of the letters 'ui', 'vi' or 'wi.' " It was afterwards sent to experts in Boston, who pronounced that it was indeed parchment inscribed with India ink that had been written with a quill pen.

For Blair and his group, the tiny fragment of parchment provided irrefutable proof of a treasure soon to be recovered. All of the people involved in the 1897 drilling operation purchased additional shares. And the physician who examined the artifact also bought shares although he had had no previous interest in the Oak Island mystery.

Many years later, Blair told the *Toronto Telegram*: "That is more convincing evidence of buried treasure than a few doubloons would be. I am satisfied that either a treasure of immense value or priceless historical documents are in a chest at the bottom of the Pit."

And so the siege continued. A third drill hole struck wood at 122 feet and then cement at 153 feet. Then the drill touched wood on one side, extending down about four feet, and cement on the other which ran an additional three feet to about 160 feet. Below the cement, the drill struck an iron barrier—immediately recognized by its sound at the surface. Two hours or more of drilling only pierced the iron one-quarter of an inch, and the attempt to drill through it was finally abandoned. Chappell states: "The clay and material at the bottom of the hole were brought up with a sand pump. A magnet was run through this material and it loaded up with fine iron cuttings thereby producing conclusive proof that it was iron we had been drilling on at 171 feet."

Two more holes were drilled, and one of them appeared to intercept a channel from which water was pumped out at the rate of about 400 gallons per minute. This suggested a second flood tunnel, probably connecting from the south shore!

Another anomaly was that most of the drilling was through soft ground (that had apparently been disturbed) and layers of blue clay. Chappell said that the clay had the "characteristics of puddled clay" (a hand worked water-tight mixture of clay, sand, and water), and was

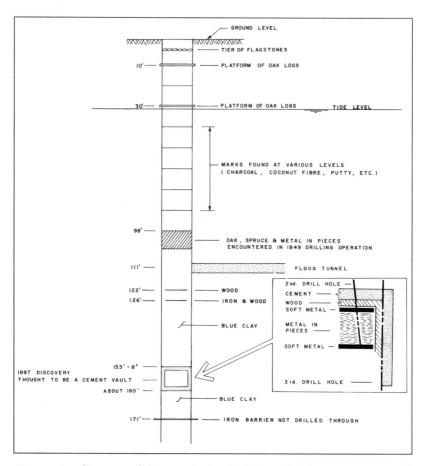

Composite diagram of discoveries in the Money Pit between 1795 and 1897.

encountered between 130 and 150 feet and, deeper still, between 160 and 171 feet.

Blair and his party were further surprised when they struck wood at 122 feet, and then wood and iron at 126 feet. No one expected to find evidence of treasure below 118 feet. The casks that collapsed into the Money Pit in 1861 were thought to have dropped to the 118-foot level. Captain Welling and his crew also believed that the casks had possibly slid into a tunnel from an adjacent shaft since the Oak Island Eldorado Company's drilling probes of 1867 left no conclusive proof that the supposed treasure had really dropped down into a cavity below. It now became evident that the casks discovered by the Truro Company in 1849 had in fact fallen much deeper into the earth.

The question arose: were the cement-like chips recovered from the borings natural, or were they man-made? Consequently, two samples were submitted in 1897 to a well-known chemical analysis firm in London, England. Without being told where the substance came from, they gave the following report:

	No. 1	No. 2
Lime (CaO)	37.40%	37.18%
Carbonate (CO_2)	33.20%	34.00%
Silica (SiO_2)	13.20%	13.92%
Iron & Alumina		
(Fe_2O_3 and Al_2O_3)	10.19%	10.13%
Moisture (at 120°C)	0.34%	0.29%
Magnesium etc.	5.67%	4.48%
	100.00%	100.00%

After receiving the report, the searchers asked the chemists' opinion as to whether the samples were natural or artificial. They replied: "From the analysis it is impossible to state definitely, but from the appearance and nature of the samples, we are of the opinion that it is a cement which has been worked by man."

The directors of the Oak Island Treasure Company became feverish to recover what appeared to be a far greater treasure than originally anticipated. The drilling work indicated that two caches were situated down in the Pit, the lower one being contained in a cement vault about seven feet high. They speculated that this chamber contained bars of gold or silver, coins and jewels, and possibly very important and valuable historical documents. Based on the drilling results and subsequent speculations, the management decided not to sell any more "outside" shares. They unanimously decided that the existing stockholders would finance the balance of the operation.

They devised a new plan to recover the treasure by sinking a shaft 175 feet to 200 feet deep and tunneling to a point below the iron obstruction at the 171-foot level in the Money Pit. This new shaft was to be used to drain the Pit by pumping, thus allowing the diggers to reach the cement vault.

Putnam selected a point about 40 feet south of the Money Pit and work got underway in October 1897. They reached a depth of 95 feet, at which point a large volume of saltwater broke in at the 70-foot level from an old shaft of the 1860s and it rose to tide level. By this time, the east end of the Island had become riddled with a labyrinth of tunnels from previous searches.

Extremely discouraged but still determined to reach the enormous fortune awaiting them in the Money Pit, Blair and his group decided to try the plan again. They selected a spot about 35 feet southwest of the abandoned shaft and about 80 feet from the Money Pit. The work began in January 1898 and continued to the first of April, when at 160 feet, saltwater again broke into the shaft through a seam of sand. Once their attempts to pump out the water failed, this shaft, too, had to be abandoned.

Incredibly, they sank four more shafts using the same approach and all ended in failure due to unsafe soil conditions, boulders, or water intrusion.

In a last-ditch effort to cope with the water entering the Money Pit, the crew ran tests to see if the flood tunnel from Smith's Cove was really clogged. They filled one of the abandoned shafts with water pumped from the shore. Soon, the muddy water fell back to sea level and, to their horror, showed up at three widely separated points near the low tide line of the south shore. No muddy water appeared at Smith's Cove. This confirmed that there was a second water channel (natural or man-made) and that the tunnel from Smith's Cove was cut off. They found similar results when water was pumped into the Money Pit and again when red dye was poured into the Pit. A fourth test consisted of lowering the water in the Money Pit and letting it settle until it was clear. They then set off a charge of dynamite near one of the south shore inlets. In a short time, the muddy water came through to the Pit. These tests were conducted in April, May, and June of 1898.

Risking ultimate failure, the Oak Island Treasure Company resumed their assault on the Money Pit in October 1899. It was enlarged to twice its size by excavating a second shaft, five feet by eight feet, alongside it on the west side. This new shaft was driven down to 113 feet where water gushed in at such an enormous force that it overwhelmed the pumps.

In 1900, further drilling operations were carried out in the Money Pit to try to learn more about the cement chamber discovered in the summer of 1897. But luck was not on their side; the auger struck boulders. Also, the cribbing was badly twisted and only the southeast corner of the Pit could be reached. They drilled to depths as great as 162 feet but struck nothing of significance.

Finally, with workmen demanding back wages, suppliers closing in to collect their bills, and liens being taken on equipment, the company collapsed. In May 1990, the Sheriff sold off most of the movable property.

For many, the personal losses were devastating—especially for those who had borrowed to buy shares. Captain John Welling lost $4,000. T. Perley Putnam had invested $20,000, much of which he had borrowed. The loss ruined him.

Frederick Blair moved to Calgary, Alberta, where he set up an insurance company of his own. He retained his treasure trove license with the Province and maintained a lease with Sophia Sellers for an annual fee of $100.

The Money Pit beckoned the adventurous, the curious, the gamblers, the rich, and the greedy. But Oak Island remained quiet for nine years, like a spider awaiting its prey.

ELEVEN

Non-pirate Treasure Bearers

O ver the first century of expeditions to recover the legendary treasure of Oak Island, new clues compounded to paint a complex picture of the original project. As the extent of knowledge about the initial undertaking grew, the idea that pirates had been the engineers slowly lost its credibility. And, as the treasure hunt moved into the 20th century, new theories were advanced to explain who built the labyrinth of pits and tunnels.

One theory that could have been the first, is that the Micmac people were responsible for the complex. Chronologically this makes sense, because the Micmac inhabited the land for hundreds of years before the arrival of the explorers and early settlers.

The Micmac lived along the coasts of Atlantic Canada where there was an abundance of fish and wildlife in the bays, coves, and rivers. They dug clams and mussels on the beaches; trapped lobsters and crabs; fished salmon, smelt, flounder, shad, skate, and eels in the shallow waters; hunted seals and collected birds' eggs on islands in the bays. In deeper water, they fished porpoise, sturgeon, small whales, and swordfish. Ducks, geese, and other birds were abundant on the seaside marshes. In the winter months, they moved inland for a short period when food became scarce and coastal living conditions grew severe. They located their winter villages beside lakes and the narrow sections of rivers where they caught fish such as salmon, trout, and eels and hunted moose, caribou, and other animals.

Some of the Micmac people camped on the shores of Mahone Bay and it is quite probable that they visited Oak Island on their hunting excursions. However, there is nothing in their history, handed down through legend, that connects them with what has been discovered on the Island. Besides, although they were clever and masterful craftsmen, the Micmac were not known to engage in heavy construction of the type evidenced on Oak Island.

If the Micmac people needed to protect anything from the explorers and early settlers, they might have taken the pains to make a place of concealment. However, there is nothing to suggest they may have had valuables or religious items that would have driven them to build the underground structures of Oak Island.

Still another theory points to the Norsemen, the first non-native people to whom the Money Pit is credited.

The Norsemen visited North America hundreds of years before Christopher Columbus arrived in 1492. Viking sagas relating the voyages of the Norse tell of Bjarni Herjolfsson's arrival in Newfoundland, around 985 A.D. A decade later, he was followed by Leif Eriksson who named the area Vinland. (The suggestion of grapes growing in that latitude has led many people to discredit Newfoundland in favor of a more southerly location such as New England, and even as far south as Florida. However, historic sources prove that wild grapes grew in Newfoundland as late as the middle of the 17th century.)

The Norsemen, who were well established in Iceland by the late ninth century A.D., settled Greenland a century later. Following the explorers and in search of Leif Eriksson's Vinland, their westward progression brought them to Atlantic Canada.

According to theory, the Norsemen established a colony in Mahone Bay. It prospered in isolation over a period of possibly 500 years, during which time it became wealthy and cultured. Then, an influenza epidemic or an Indian attack all but decimated the colony. Finding that they could no longer remain in their reduced numbers, the survivors made plans to return to their motherland. Due to a shortage of room on board their only ship, they were obliged to hide their valuables and the chronicles of their settlement's history. Figuring that they or their descendents would return, they buried everything of recoverable worth on Oak Island. They set sail but were lost in a storm, and they vanished into history without further mention.

The theory is intriguing but it lacks archaeological evidence that there ever was a Norse settlement in Mahone Bay. Furthermore, there is nothing to be found in saga tales to support this hypothesis. Also, the coconut fiber uncovered at Smith's Cove indicates a deposit by someone from a tropical climate. For these reasons, the relationship between the Norse and Oak Island seems highly unlikely.

Aside from the Micmac and the non-indigenous Norse, a long-standing popular theory connects Oak Island with France and the great fortress of Louisbourg.

Following the English claim to Atlantic Canada in 1497 when John Cabot landed on Nova Scotia's Cape Breton Island, France attempted to establish ownership of this part of the new world. In 1605, Samuel de Champlain established a permanent settlement at Port Royal, on the Bay of Fundy. Then, in 1621, the English laid claim to the territory, claiming that Cabot planted the first English flag. For almost a century and a half, England and France continued to wage wars over the ownership of the new land.

After losing the War of the Spanish Succession, France signed the Treaty of Utrecht in 1713 and began construction of the huge fortress of Louisbourg on Cape Breton Island, about 240 miles north of Oak Island. By the terms of the treaty, France had lost most of her colonies in Atlantic Canada, retaining only the islands of Prince Edward, Cape Breton, St. Pierre, and Miquelon. The fortress was built to protect the remaining colonies.

The Louisbourg fortifications were huge, covering about 50 acres of land surrounding the town. Built by engineers, artisans, and private contractors from France with labor supplied by French troops, it was completed in 1744 at a cost of millions of dollars.

In 1745 the British captured the fort after a 49-day siege but it was returned to France, three years later, by the Treaty of Aix-la-Chapelle.

Ten years later, in 1758, it was again seized by the British and two years later it was completely demolished to make certain that it would never again be of any value to France.

The theory contends that during the construction of the fortress, the French government was afraid to retain within the town the huge sums of money required to pay for the work because of the constant threat of war with Britain. So, they selected the isolated and well-hidden Oak Island to serve as a repository, engaging professional engineers and military labor in the construction of the works.

Another theory suggests that Oak Island was hardly a government project. Rather, the treasure belonged to a dishonest contractor or a high-ranking French official who funneled royal treasury funds off French pay ships en route to Louisbourg during the construction of the fort. The money (gold and silver) was to be recovered after the fortress was completed but the embezzler and his cohorts were killed in one of the skirmishes with the British.

A third theory is that a French pay ship floundered off the shores of Oak Island when it struck a shoal while being driven into the Bay by a vicious storm. Her crew buried her cargo of coin and bullion on the Island, either dishonestly or to protect it from the British. However, this fanciful speculation falls flat on its face in view of known facts. The French pay ship *Chameau* was the only vessel reported lost and she was recovered by divers in 1965. She went down on a shoal near Louisbourg in 1725 with about $750,000 in pay on board.

A popular speculation establishing a French connection with Oak Island involves the great armada of the Duc d'Anville.

In 1746, a year after losing the fortress of Louisbourg to the British, France assembled a huge fleet of 65 ships, carrying over 3,000 troops, to retake their lost stronghold in the new world and regain their foothold in Atlantic Canada.

The armada, commanded by the Duc d'Anville, encountered troubles almost all the way across the Atlantic. Ships were lost in storms and diseases broke out among the crews. Then it ran into a violent storm off Nova Scotia's Sable Island (known as the graveyard of the Atlantic) and most of the fleet was lost.

D'Anville's flagship and a few others dropped anchor in Halifax Harbour (then called Chebucto Harbour) where D'Anville and many of his men died of various diseases resulting from the pestilence that had broken out on numerous ships during the Atlantic crossing.

Ships of the fleet are said to have been widely separated during the storm and it is speculated that a payship of what remained of the great armada found its way into Mahone Bay and her cargo of gold and silver was buried on Oak Island.

As enticing as the theory is, it has no evidence in its support. Although one or more ships could have strayed into Mahone Bay after being separated from the fleet, historians say that there is no record that any of the vessels carried "specie or bullion."

One theory that has captured the imaginations of many is that the Acadians constructed the underground works of Oak Island.

The settlers of a colony established by Samuel de Champlain in 1605 at Port Royal on the Bay of Fundy were the first of a people now known as the "Acadians." These people grew in numbers and their communities spread along the Bay of Fundy and the Minas Basin where they farmed the fertile lands and became engaged in fishing and commerce.

The Acadians were a peaceful people and strived to remain neutral during the 140-year period of British and French skirmishes that followed the 1621 British claim of ownership based on Cabot's landing in 1497.

After the Treaty of Utrecht in 1713, by which Britain acquired most of France's colonies in the new world, the Acadians were pressured to take an oath of alliance to British rule which included the bearing of arms against France in times of conflict. The Acadians resisted the demand and won a concession whereby they signed an oath of alliance to the British Crown but with the condition that they would remain neutral if France tried to take over the territory and a war ensued.

In 1749, a year after the fortress of Louisbourg and Cape Breton Island were returned to France by the treaty of Aix-la-Chapelle, Edward Cornwallis became the governor of mainland Nova Scotia, which included the lands occupied by the Acadians.

By the time Cornwallis was appointed governor, the Acadian population had grown to around 10,000. This relatively large number troubled Cornwallis considerably because it represented a threat to British control. Although the Acadians had signed an oath of neutrality, Cornwallis feared that they would assist France in a future attempt to reclaim her lost territory. If he evicted them, they would only move north to Cape Breton Island and increase France's strength in that portion of the new land. The only way to secure Britain's position was to alter the existing oath to one of unconditional allegiance.

However, the Acadians refused to alter the oath and the uneasy condition remained until 1755 (three years prior to the final siege of Louisbourg) when the British began expelling them from the Province. Approximately 6,000 Acadians were driven from Nova Scotia in that year. Most of those remaining were expelled in the following couple of years. Entire villages were cleared out and the people shipped to places along the Atlantic coast as far south as Georgia. Many found their way to Louisiana where the name "Cajun" now signifies the origin of the French descendents.

The theory has been advanced that a group of Acadians anticipated the expulsion several years prior to 1755 and took positive action to preserve their valuables. They gathered up an enormous amount of gold and silver and transported it by ship to Mahone Bay. Once there, they constructed the elaborate works found on Oak Island to prevent the British from confiscating their accumulated fortunes.

The Acadians may have reached a point of substantial affluency. Some conducted trading businesses as well as smuggling operations. They sold supplies to their fellow Frenchmen at Louisbourg and also carried on commerce with the English garrisons on mainland Nova Scotia. Some Acadians sold supplies to pirates. Their industrious activities brought in "hard currency" but it is difficult to imagine an amount sufficiently large to justify the Oak Island undertaking.

An enchanting but historically insupportable theory involves the crown jewels of France.

On June 20, 1791, Louis XIV and Marie Antoinette fled Paris with a mob of revolutionaries in hot pursuit. Their destination was Austria where they planned to seek a permanent refuge.

The crown jewels of France vanished along with Louis and Marie. The couple was captured a few days later in Varennes but the jewels along with their own collection of valuables were missing.

It was rumored that a lady-in-waiting accompanied Louis XIV and Marie Antoinette when they tried to escape and that she was later seen in Louisbourg. According to the tale, the jewels were smuggled to

Marie Antoinette's crown jewels disappeared in 1791 and are said to have been smuggled to Louisbourg.

Surrender of Louisbourg, 1758.

Louisbourg by the lady-in-waiting or by an engineer reputed to have been Marie Antoinette's lover. From there, the jewels were shipped to Mahone Bay and buried on Oak Island.

The theory is severely flawed by the fact that Louisbourg was captured by the British in 1758 and completely demolished in 1760 (more than 30 years before the flight and capture of Louis and Marie).

The crown jewels did disappear but not to Oak Island. Prior to his attempted escape, the King sent the jewels by a trusted courier to Brussels so they could then be forwarded to a special agent in Austria. The jewels were later seized by the French Government.

Some theories appear to be based on the simple fact that treasures disappeared and have never been found. One in particular involves a vast amount of gold, silver ecclesiastical plate, and statues that disappeared from England in the 17th century.

Frederick Blair was especially partial to the lost treasure concept and speculated thus: "One of the most reasonable explanations of the treasure is that it is the royal and church plate and valuables known to have been removed from England and hidden during the Protectorate of Cromwell after the execution of Charles I. This treasure simply vanished from the face of the earth and has never been recovered. Very probably it now lies buried on Oak Island. If so, its value will far exceed, for archaeological and historical purposes, anything in the way of bullion or more precious metal."

Another "disappearance" theory espouses that the lost treasure of St. Andrew's Cathedral in Scotland is buried on Oak Island.

According to tradition, an enormous quantity of ecclesiastical plate, gold, silver, and gems mysteriously disappeared from the ancient Cathedral in 1560. The treasure trove is thought to partly include spoils taken from the English following the Battle of Bannockburn in 1314.

Several searches were made in the Cathedral ruins in the late 19th and early 20th centuries but no trace of a treasure was found. However, a couple of secret tunnels were discovered beneath the ruins, leading to the conjecture that the monks had removed the valuables to another location in Scotland or perhaps out of the country altogether.

The hypothesis holds that the monks carried off the treasure and

Battle of Bannockburn, 1314. The spoils, stored in St. Andrew's Cathedral, disappeared in 1560.

transported it all the way across the Atlantic to Nova Scotia. Presumably, they scouted the coastline for the most appropriate inlet, found Mahone Bay, and selected Oak Island. One proponent of the theory stated: "Priests [monks] from the Abbey of St. Andrew's took their gold plate and other treasures over to Oak Island in 1745, after the defeat of Prince Charles at Culloden. Nova Scotia was a wilderness then, of course. I spent three months at St. Andrew's years ago, trying to find what had been done with the stuff. Their journals were all written in old Latin, but I got the hang of it. The lot that sailed away never got home...."

These historically-related whodunit theories of the early 1900s appear to fall into two distinct categories: those that are impossible to consider because they are historically unsupportable, and those that are untenable due to insufficient or conflicting evidence. The latter present a greater problem because one is driven to ask the question, "Could that have really happened?"

Recent discoveries suggest that real whodunits will make an appearance but they are far different from the early non-pirate theories.

TWELVE

Franklin D. Roosevelt's Fascination

Not surprisingly, the Oak Island mystery sparked the imagination and enthusiasm of many 20th century dignitaries. In 1940, film actor Errol Flynn attempted to head up an expedition to recover the elusive Oak Island treasure. Although he had previously failed in two other treasure hunts in the Caribbean and Alaska, he wanted to try once again on Oak Island. But his enthusiasm was dampened when he learned that another treasure hunter controlled the search rights. In 1970, movie star John Wayne was an owner of Statesman Mining Company of Aspen, Colorado. His mining firm approached Triton Alliance, an Oak Island treasure search company, regarding a piece of excavation equipment they were interested in leasing to Triton. The search company obtained the equipment and there was talk of having Wayne narrate a documentary film on Oak Island. For reasons unknown—perhaps Wayne's heavy workload— nothing came of it.

Another unlikely Oak Island enthusiast was Franklin D. Roosevelt,

84

U.S. president, Franklin D. Roosevelt, (1882–1945), joined the Old Gold Salvage group, formed to find the Oak Island treasure.

who was destined to become president of the United States.

From the age of three, Roosevelt spent almost every summer of his childhood and teenage years on Campobello, a narrow ten-mile long island in the Canadian waters of the Bay of Fundy, off the coast of Maine. There, his father had built a comfortable seaside cottage, and Roosevelt learned, by the age of six, the rudiments of sailing on his large yacht. When he was 16, Roosevelt received the gift of a 21-foot sailboat from his father. He named her the *New Moon* and sailed her almost daily at Campobello, learning the location of shoals and the art of navigation.

It was around this stage in his life that Roosevelt began to exhibit a keen interest in treasure hunting. He and a Groton prep-school roommate sailed from the Roosevelt summer home on Campobello Island to nearby Grand Manan Island, in the Bay of Fundy, in search of a treasure chest that had supposedly been buried by Captain William Kidd. Roosevelt and his companion spent four days searching for the cache but found nothing except an old plank with the initials "W.K." etched on its surface. The initials are thought to have been the work of a prankster playing a practical joke on anyone who might be searching for Kidd's legendary treasure.

As a boy, Roosevelt first heard stories about Oak Island from the people of Campobello Island when he spent his summer vacations there with his mother. He undoubtedly dreamed of going to Oak Island and joining the search but it wasn't until 1909 at the age of 27 that he gained the opportunity to become actively involved. At that time he was a law clerk with the New York firm of Carter, Ledyard, and Milburn.

Roosevelt joined a treasure search group headed by Captain Henry L. Bowdoin, a charismatic engineer with a flair for adventure.

Bowdoin was convinced that he could recover the long-sought treasure with the application of heavy equipment and divers. He created a renewed interest in the search through a series of interviews that appeared in New York, Boston, and Nova Scotia newspapers. Bowdoin was described as a mining, mechanical, and marine engineer, a master marine pilot, and a licensed submarine diver. He was credited with a broad range of expertise, including dredging harbors and building bridges. Bowdoin said, "Modern machinery and engineering science will solve in a jiffy the difficulties Captain Kidd made to guard his treasure."

Confident of his ability to succeed, Bowdoin boasted, "Any competent engineer could clear up that affair in no time. And I don't want more than two weeks for the work, after I get my machinery and crew on the ground. It will be a vacation and about all I stand to lose is the wages of the men and my own time, for the machinery will be valuable in my business afterward. I am not going to organize a company, though I may take a personal friend or two into the enterprise."

In April 1909, Bowdoin formed the Old Gold Salvage and Wrecking Company, with offices at 44 Broadway in New York. The firm's authorized capital was $250,000, divided into a public offering of shares at one dollar each. The officers of the company were: Henry L. Bowdoin, president; Frederick Blair, vice-president; L.H. Andrews, a New York attorney, treasurer; G.D. Mosher, a New York accountant, secretary; Captain John W. Welling, member of the board of directors.

The Company's prospectus was comprehensive and impressive. It read: "Over one hundred years ago a treasure, estimated to be over ten million dollars [basis of estimate unknown], was buried on Oak Island, in Mahone Bay, Nova Scotia, supposedly by pirates, who took such pains to safeguard it, that although numerous attempts have been made to recover it, it lies undisturbed to this day. These failures were due to lack of modern machinery and ignorance; each expedition being stopped by water and lack of funds. The pirates connected the pit in which the treasure was buried with the ocean by an underground tunnel, so that when buried and the tunnel opened, *the water level was sixty feet above the treasure*. The diggers in the pit, which is quite a distance from the shore, have invariably been driven out by this water which is *salt*, and rises and falls with the tide. As a pit was dug near the money pit 110-feet deep without striking any water, yet became flooded when they tunneled into the money pit, it proves the existence of an underground connection between the pit and the ocean. The location of this tunnel has been practically determined, but as yet no one has known how to cut it off.

"That there really is some sort of treasure there has been verified by gold shavings and part of a watch chain brought up with borings from crude implements used. Since these borings were made, the parties have made regular payments on a lease of the property, which gives them the exclusive right to any treasure that may be found, which lease has been further augmented by a Government permit.

"Believing, from the above, and from other facts, that a treasure of *some value* is buried in the pit on Oak Island, Nova Scotia, and knowing that with modern methods of machinery, the recovery of that treasure is *easy*, ridiculously easy, an exclusive contract has been entered into with the owners and leaseholders of the property, for its recovery."

Bowdoin proposed locating the supposed treasure by drilling; then locating the flood tunnel by boring a series of holes parallel and near the shore at Smith's Cove; blocking off the tunnel by driving sheet piling across it (on this project, sheet piling would have been interlocking sheets of steel driven vertically into the ground); excavating holes into the tunnel on both the shore and inland sides of the piling, and finally pumping the inland hole dry. After blocking off the tunnel, he proposed to move his large excavation bucket to the Money Pit and, with the aid of a 1,000-gallon-per-minute pump, recover the "treasure."

Conceding that this approach might fail, Bowdoin offered this alternative: "Should, however, the tunnel *not* be located; the pump *not* be able to keep out the water, and the bucket *not* bring up all of the treasure, some, perhaps having slipped to one side, then, and in that event one of 'Bowdoin's Air Lock Caissons' could be placed in the pit, sunk through water or earth to any depth desired, and side tubes forced out to reach any desired spot. Compressed air keeps out all water and allows men to work at the bottom, and send any articles up and out through the air lock. The caisson is now used in sinking foundations through earth and water to bedrock; for foundations of buildings and *through* the water of a river and to bedrock beneath its bed; for foundations for bridges, piers, etc. *The treasure can positively be recovered by its use.*"

The prospectus ends by addressing future company plans following the work on Oak Island, and by summarizing its objectives. "The wide publicity given by the press of the intention of Mr. Bowdoin to recover this Oak Island Treasure has resulted in the receipt of a number of letters calling attention to other treasures and valuables that could be recovered through scientific modern equipment. Several of these are of exceptional interest, being valuable, non-perishable cargoes of vessels, and sunken valuables, the locations of which are known.

"As no systematic, scientific efforts have been made to recover and salvage the more or less valuable cargoes, etc., of wrecks which are piling up at the rate of over one hundred a year, it is deemed good business policy to get together a complete modern equipment, and after the recovery of the treasure at Oak Island, to utilize said equipment in a general salvage and wrecking business.

"To this end *The Old Gold Salvage and Wrecking Company* has been formed, and has taken up the matter on a *cold, business basis.* The objects of the Company are:

"*First*: To recover, by use of modern methods, the Ten Million Dollars buried on Oak Island, Nova Scotia.

"*Second*: To then use the machinery and equipment purchased for the salvage and wrecking of sunken vessels known to contain gold and valuable cargo.

"The lease and Government permit, under which the recovery of the treasure will be made, are now controlled by the Company.

"The officers and directors of the Company are practical men; well versed in pneumatic and general wrecking operations, who will be on the ground and superintend operations for the recovery of the treasure.

"The recovery of the treasure would yield a dividend of 4,000 percent on the entire capital stock; and, as operations should begin in May or June and be completed in three or four weeks, should be available this summer. This will leave time for the salvage of an exceptionally valuable cargo before next winter, when the plant would operate in southern waters, where certain other valuables await our attention.

"To purchase the equipment, stock is now offered to the general public at a popular price, $1.00 per share. No order for less than ten shares will be accepted."

Roosevelt was apparently attracted by the newspaper articles about Bowdoin and impressed with the prospectus of The Old Gold Salvage and Wrecking Company. He and three of his friends, Duncan G. Harris, Albert Gallatin, and John W. Shields, purchased shares in the Company and visited Oak Island during Bowdoin's expedition. Roosevelt himself visited the Island several times during the summer of 1909.

Despite the confidence and expertise that Bowdoin radiated, he was only able to raise $5,000 through the sale of shares but Frederick Blair helped by granting the Company a two-year lease in exchange for his shares.

With all the confidence gained through engineering training and experience, Bowdoin was certain that he would succeed. He set sail from New York on August 18, 1909. After purchasing extra equipment in Halifax, they arrived at Oak Island on August 27th and set up their operation which was dubbed "Camp Kidd."

After an unsuccessful attempt to locate the flood tunnel entrance at Smith's Cove, Bowdoin made a direct assault on the Money Pit. All obstructions such as platforms and ladders were ripped out using the excavation bucket to a depth of 113 feet. Due to the lack of funds, the Company had been unable to purchase the proposed 1,000-gallon-per-minute pump. The water level in the Pit stood 30 feet below the ground surface. When a diver was lowered down to the bottom of the Pit to report on the conditions of the cribbing, the report was discouraging. The cribbing was in a terrible state. It was twisted and badly out of alignment. The bottom was covered with a mess of tangled planks; timbers were "sticking up in all directions."

Bowdoin then resorted to conventional drilling. More than two dozen borings were made to depths as great as 171 feet without encountering a trace of treasure.

By this time Bowdoin had exhausted all of the funds and the operation was closed down in November.

Roosevelt had probably joined the expedition more for the adventure and romance of treasure hunting than for the expectation of financial gain because he kept in contact with his 1909 fellow searchers for a period spanning 30 years. His personal records include letters regarding Oak Island that date as late as 1939 when he was serving his second term as president of the United States.

That a man of Roosevelt's intelligence and wisdom retained an interest in the Oak Island enigma for the better part of his life is a testament to the depth of one of the world's most baffling mysteries.

THIRTEEN

Oak Island Folklore

T he early settlers brought numerous superstitions of European origin to Nova Scotia which were associated with buried treasure. The province, connected to New Brunswick by a neck of land only 15 miles wide, is almost an island. Its coastline stretches over 1,000 miles. The coast is indented with hundreds of bays and coves, many of which made excellent hiding places for pirates in the early days. The settlers were imaginative. They envisaged buried treasures on the beaches and in the woodlands bordering the shores. They blended their fancies with their superstitions and a wealth of folklore was born.

Oak Island is prominent in the folklore, and the legend of pirates and buried treasure is deeply embedded in the collective consciousness of the people of Chester and the Mahone Bay area. An imitation treasure chest filled with costume jewelry and sundry items is displayed in a shop window; a manikin pirate garbed in rubber boots, holding a sword and wearing the proverbial black patch over one eye, stands guard beside the entrance of a gift shop; a sign advertising Oak Island tours displays a pirate carrying a chest on his right shoulder; restaurant and beverage lounges operate under names such as "The Pirate Lure Beverage Room Grill" and "Cap'n Kidd's Lounge."

The Bay is named after pirate tradition. The name "Mahone" is derived from the Turkish word "mahone" meaning "a low-lying craft, propelled by long oars, called sweepers, and much used by pirates in early days of the Mediterranean."

Oak Island is steeped in superstition and shrouded with stories of the supernatural based on piracy. Perhaps the spookiest story is the one about pirates who create a ghost to guard a treasure. According to legend, the pirate crew, when burying a cache, would stand around the hole into which a chest had been lowered and the captain would exclaim, "Who is going to stay and guard the treasure?" Being a greedy lot, the pirates would compete verbally for the assignment, each hoping to be chosen so that he could keep the treasure for himself once the captain and his crew departed. One voice crying, "I will" would naturally ring out louder than the rest, and the captain would identify that particular pirate, approach him and say, "You've got the job." That evening, the captain would throw a big party with loads of rum and all the crew would get roaring drunk and dance around a huge bonfire. Towards the end of the evening when most of the crew had passed out and the others were bordering on comatose, the captain would bludgeon the sozzled volunteer and push him into the pit on top of the treasure chest. The captain would then order a handful of staggering drunks, still able to function, to shovel the earth back into the hole, thus leaving a ghost behind to guard the treasure.

There are various twists as to how a pirate was selected to remain as a ghost. According to another version, an unsuspecting stranger was taken ashore along with a few men and he innocently volunteered thinking that he would retrieve the ill-gotten spoils for himself as soon as the pirate ship sailed away. And, another version says that the pirates gathered together on the beach around the open pit into which the treasure chest had been lowered and drew lots to determine who should be murdered and buried with the cache. The "winner" would either be decapitated by the crew or buried alive with the treasure. An even more gruesome yarn suggests that the captain would select a man at random, cut off his head, and toss it into the pit on top of the treasure to watch it.

An alternative to the ghost of a pirate guarding a treasure on Oak

Island is the legend that "a dog with fiery eyes" guards the treasure of Captain Kidd which many believe lies buried on the Island. According to this story, the dog has "blood red eyes that glow like hot coals" and is thought to be the Devil's watchdog. Others believe that the dog is the ghost of a pirate who was sacrificed to the Money Pit.

Harris Joudrey who lived his first ten years on Oak Island claimed to have seen the dog when he was a boy of nine, in 1900. According to Joudrey, the large dog was sitting on the sill of a door to the "boiler house" of the Money Pit. The dog had never been seen before on the Island. The animal watched young Joudrey and some of his companions as they walked by and disappeared from sight, and he was never seen again. The incident scared the "daylights" out of Joudrey and his friends.

In another version of the legend, a lady relative of Anthony Graves, the Graves who owned most or all of Oak Island, was "scared stiff" by a dog as large as a small horse or colt. The encounter was on the north side of the Island and the relative witnessed the huge dog disappear into the side of a stone wall that marked one of the property boundary lines.

We are repeatedly told that the belief in ghosts guarding buried treasure made it difficult for early Oak Island expeditions to recruit workmen. Oak Island is said to have been viewed with a superstitious eye by all of the residents of Chester, and there are many curious stories related to the Island.

According to folklore, a light might indicate the place where a treasure is buried and one story tells of a bright light appearing on Oak Island and illuminating the Money Pit. Men are seen burying a treasure in the glow of the light. The phenomenon is said to be "looking back into time," as if the light were functioning as a time machine bringing the past forward for a brief observation.

The belief that ghostly lights seen at night usually indicates that a treasure has been buried nearby is supported by another Nova Scotia tale. According to rumor, when a chest of doubloons (sometimes called "double loons" by early storytellers) was discovered at Port Medway, a light hung in the air above the place where it was found. Nevertheless, the doubloons were delivered to a bank and exchanged for a large sum of money.

That light is associated with buried treasure is further supported by another piece of folklore. Many locals believe that treasure is buried on

Tancook Island, in Mahone Bay, and that a bright light has often been seen there before a storm.

One family is said to have been so terrified by the light on Oak Island that they were driven to move, never to return. Mrs. Rollande Coleman of Ontario who lived on the mainland opposite Oak Island in the early 1980s tells of seeing a bright light over the Island. She and her two daughters, Rhonda and Leslie, were sitting beside a large window facing the Island when the incident occurred. In a telephone interview on January 8, 1992, Mrs. Coleman said the light was large and bright, as the light from a flash camera seen up close, but with a longer period of illumination. "It happened one summer evening between 6:30 and 7:00," Mrs. Coleman recalled. "The skies were clear and it was not flash lightning. Rhonda and I ran outside to see what was going on. We first thought that an aircraft was in trouble and trying to ditch somewhere on or near the Island. Leslie saw it too." Mrs. Coleman doesn't profess to have any theory to explain the light. She simply holds to the description of what she saw and says, "I can't explain it. I can only tell you what we saw." Mrs. Coleman does, however, confess that she and her daughters were both mesmerized and puzzled by what they had witnessed.

Besides the prescriptions for locating buried treasure, there is a rule to be followed once the digging begins. According to superstition, a treasure will disappear if a single word is spoken.

In some instances an unlucky accident or encounter has caused someone to speak and the treasure was lost. A story from folklore tells of a group of people digging for treasure one night on an unnamed tract of land which appears to be the eastern end of Oak Island. The diggers arrived at the treasure site with lanterns and spades and set about digging, taking special care not to utter a word. Finally, one of them exclaimed, "There it is!" and the treasure vanished.

Some folklorists say that a spoken word gives the guardian ghost power to act on his own accord and anything may happen. According to legend, one group of searchers actually found a treasure chest but one of them spoke, thus breaking the forbidden rule. In all these instances, the men are said to have dropped their shovels and run for their lives.

A lady from Mahone Bay told me of another superstition that claimed if someone spoke while digging for treasure, the pit would fill with frogs. She said that her great grandfather and several other men went out to dig for a buried treasure at full moon. The men began digging at midnight. By three in the morning they had reached a depth of ten feet. Then, one of the men accidentally jabbed the tip of his spade into the tip of one of his toes. The instantaneous shock of pain caused him to forget the code of silence for a split second and he howled an ear-splitting profanity. A moment later, the pit filled to the top with "green" frogs and all the men were smothered to death. Only the lady's great grandfather escaped. He had left the pit for a few minutes to fetch a jug of drinking water for the men. As he was about to step on the top rung of the ladder leading to the bottom of the pit, he heard the fatal words.

In addition to the instruction to keep quiet when digging for treasure and the severe consequences that can otherwise occur, a bizarre suggestion about how to recover a treasure has spread "like wildfire."

Sometime around the middle of the 19th century, the superstition was circulated that a treasure would rise to the surface if a live baby was thrown into the pit. At about that time, a man who immediately became dubbed the "Bogeyman of Lunenburg" arrived as if from nowhere. The man, who had arrived in Lunenburg by schooner, walked the streets of the town asking people where he could find Oak Island. He apparently was looking for work and had heard that an expedition on the Island was hiring workmen. Somehow, the rumor immediately spread that the stranger was searching for a baby to throw into the Money Pit and, if not a baby, then possibly any helpless child. Terror consumed all of the mothers with small children, and doors and windows were bolted, barred, and nailed shut. A young boy who had heard the rumor slipped out of his house and went in search of the stranger, through curiosity. The boy walked for a long time and eventually ended up a couple of miles on the outskirts of town. Dusk was approaching so the boy turned around and headed back towards home. On his way back he encountered the stranger at a turn in the road. The little boy's curiosity suddenly turned to terror. The gravity of the rumor took hold when he viewed the stranger's uncomely appearance. The boy fled from the road into the woods and became lost. That night, the men of the town went in search of the stranger, expecting to catch him with the supposed abducted child. They found the "Bogeyman" early that evening as he sauntered along the downtown waterfront, but he had no child in tow. Meanwhile, the disoriented little boy, who had been floundering around the woods in circles, luckily stumbled back onto the road. He recognized certain landmarks along the road and arrived at his parents' back door near midnight.

Another version of the "Bogeyman of Lunenburg" says that in his effort to find a baby, he "went about frightening all the little boys and girls wherever he went." However, it is doubtful that a man "really" roamed about the Town of Lunenburg "purposefully" trying to steal a baby to give to an Oak Island search party.

Oak Island-inspired visions form an integral part of the local folklore. One popular legend tells of the specter of men dressed in red jackets.

One man is said to have been digging on Oak Island but for reasons unknown, he was obliged to temporarily discontinue his work. When he resumed, he was interrupted by a man in a red coat who told him that he was "not digging in the right place." The red-coated man then dematerialized by disappearing into the bottom of the Pit.

In 1940, a little girl living with her parents on Oak Island reportedly saw men at Smith's Cove wearing red jackets. She was scared and crying when she came running into the house so her father went down to the shore to investigate. There was no one there. Furthermore, it was in the winter and there was snow on the ground but there wasn't a trace of a footprint anywhere.

Another vision involves what has become locally known as the "Ancient Man." Anthony Graves' son William saw this apparition in the 1850s when he was out in his boat one evening trapping lobsters on the north side of Oak Island. The "Ancient Man" was seated between a couple of trees near the shore. Displaying long whiskers, the apparition called to William, saying, "Come here and I will give you all the gold you can carry." William didn't take the specter up on his offer. He was so frightened that he rowed away from the Island as fast as his oars would propel him. When William encountered the "Ancient Man," he was in his twenties. At that time he was very ill and dying of tuberculosis. He told the story of the "Ancient Man" while on his deathbed.

In another instance of Oak Island-inspired visions, a visitor to the Money Pit witnessed the murder of a Spanish monk. The victim had his throat cut and was buried in a subterranean tomb. During the vision, the tourist went into a trance, and ended up rolling around on the ground, screaming.

And then there is an alternative suggestion for finding the treasure: "Throw a black person into the Money Pit." Knowledge of this tradition sparked an awesome vision for a visitor to the Island from Kingston, Ontario. In 1984, the visitor, D. Dawwber, wrote me:

"Two years ago my family and I visited Oak Island. While there I had an experience which may be of help to those working there. Walking back from the diggings, on the road, toward the car park, just over the crest of the hill, I had what I can only describe as a very strong impression. I am a very practical, down-to-earth person but the impression I had was of a dark face, in some distress, in a dark place. I didn't quite know what to make of it. Driving back to the campsite, I told my family about it.

"Lately, helping my son prepare a school speech about Oak Island, we were browsing through your book and that of V.H. Harris [R.V. Harris]. I came across the theory that the treasure, or whatever, is buried above water level and that the workers had tunneled upward into the hill to do so. Also was mentioned an old custom of burying a dark person with it. The experience I had on Oak Island came flooding back.

"It is such a coincidence that, scepticism on my part aside, I write to tell you of it. If it is of no help, no matter. If it helps solve the mystery, all to the good."

Oak Island legends are numerous and these stories only scratch the surface. The folklore is as deep as the mystery that engulfs the Money Pit.

FOURTEEN

Legendary Maps

O ver the past 100 years, people have placed great faith in the validity of maps and charts to provide details about Oak Island and the Money Pit. Each of these maps has an interesting story behind it and investigators of the mystery show no signs of exhausting the possibilities of interpretation.

The first map was brought to the attention of the public in a story published in the *Boston Traveller* on December 26, 1893, and in the *Halifax Evening Mail* on January 3, 1894. It was a story about a map found 67 years previously, giving precise information about a treasure buried on an island on the southeastern coast of Nova Scotia that had been frequented by pirates. The author of the story was a man by the name of J. Edward Wilson who wrote in a letter that he had been in New Brunswick in 1886 to visit an elderly relative in his 80s, who told him the following:

"When a young man of about 20 years of age, and that is a long time ago, I was working in a shipyard when one day a sailor came into the yard. He was evidently from a foreign ship that had arrived to load deal [fir or pine timber] as the place was a great resort then for ships in the lumber trade. He was a man of about 50 years of age, large, heavy, dark, and swarthy. I entered into conversation with him. He said that he was anxious to raise some money to enable him to get to Boston; that if I would advance, say, $20 he in return would give me a valuable secret of where there was an immense amount of money buried. It being about the time when one heard of finds that were being made of valuables that had been hidden during the French troubles and also the American war, I at once 'caught on' as the saying is. It was then arranged that he would come and sleep in my room that night, as there was a spare bed there, which he accordingly did.

"He then told me something of his history; that he had been a pirate and in later years a privateer, and that now as the latter occupation was about played out he was getting weary and wanted to get home to his native country, Spain; that if he could get to Boston he would stand a better chance of finding a ship going there. He showed a plan which he said had come into his possession, and the meaning of which he could clearly explain. It was of an island of a certain form, situated on the southeastern coast of Nova Scotia and was once the rendezvous of pirates, and that a large amount of treasure was buried there. On this island was a certain oak tree, from a branch of which hung a large ship's block that [was] used in sinking a deep shaft, the bottom of which communicated with the sea level by a tunnel. The shaft had been filled up as being of no further use, as the exit for the removal of the treasure would be through the tunnel. But for reasons unknown to him the treasure was never put there, but buried only 20 feet from the surface, at a certain distance from the tree, naming the distance, where it would be safer from the inquisitive intruder than if it were at the bottom of the shaft, the most likely place to look for it. And then it may have been the original intention of the depositor that the shaft was intended for a blind, for who would not be deceived under such conditions?

"When the sailor had finished his story I, as you can imagine, was worked up to a high pitch of curiosity to find out where this wonderful island was; but on this point hinged our bargain. When I paid him the money, he was then to give the name and directions how to find the island, also to mark on the plan the exact course by compass from the tree to where the treasure lay buried; so having found the island, then the tree with the course and distance given, it would be an easy matter to find the spot, when a few days digging would reveal the wonderful collection of untold wealth. Yes, of course I would agree to his offer and the money would be forthcoming the next day.

"Sleep that night was long delayed; it was to dream of finding the precious coins and feasting my eyes on the glittering gold. The next day however, when I came to look at the matter from various points of reason, my ardour cooled somewhat. The story seemed too good to be true. It savoured too much of the improbable; besides it was a good deal of money for me to raise at that time. So I wavered all day, undecided what to do, until the following day. When that day came the sailor disappeared as suddenly as he had come. I learned that he left in a vessel for Eastport and from there to Boston.

"When my short-lived vision of wealth had passed, I was compelled to stick to the broadaxe as the most reliable instrument to hew out a future. But in after years I had occasion to regret my want of decision, when I heard of parties who were digging for treasure on Oak Island which corresponded in so many points to that described by the pirate sailor. I have long since arrived at the belief of his story and that it is one and the same place."

Wilson's relative said that the pirate sailor didn't connect Captain Kidd with the buried treasure. Furthermore, he placed the date of the original project at the close of the 18th century—long after Kidd was executed. According to Wilson, the relative "attributed considerable importance to a large rock as being an important landmark, but my memory does not serve me sufficiently to say anything about it."

On one hand, Wilson's story seems incredible. Why didn't the sailor who professed to know the name and location of the island go there and retrieve the treasure for himself? Why would he forfeit an enormous treasure for $20? But on the other hand, the story contains a fragment of credibility. A large granite boulder on the beach at Joudrey's Cove later proved to be a piece of the Oak Island puzzle. Also, the statement that a treasure was buried in a location divorced from the Money Pit is a popular theory of modern investigators.

It has been suggested that someone may have invented the story after reading the 1893 Oak Island Treasure Company prospectus. But for what reason would Wilson concoct such a tale? Does the suggestion imply that he was paid by someone to write the letter to further the sale of shares?

This newspaper article went unknown by Frederick Blair until he was made aware of it in the summer of 1916. Blair is said to have searched for Wilson without success. Whether or not the map is fact or fiction will probably never be known.

The legend of the dying sailor revealing the location of a buried treasure has always been popular and a 1909 essay by a Mahone Bay school-teacher tells how Simeon Lynds of the 1803–1804 Onslow search party became involved. He obtained a map from the descendent of an old man who had told a story on his sickbed concerning the burying of pirate treasure. The story relates:

"Lynds became interested through a paper that was brought to light in a peculiar way. Somewhere in Virginia there lived a very old man who on his sickbed told his son, himself a man of 70, where in an old sea chest he would find a piece of paper that might reveal some buried treasure on an island somewhere up north that the old man's father had helped to bury with many others who had been compelled to work under an armed guard, under the pirate Kidd. This old man had joined Kidd's company to save his life, and after working a long time, the treasure was buried at a great depth on an oak-covered island. And when the hole was nearly filled up, he and another man, fearing they would be killed when the work was done, decided they would endeavor to escape. And one very stormy night mid [sic] rain and a gale of wind, they made their way to the shore, swam to the mainland and wandered on and on [sic]. After some time his companion took sick and died. But after weeks of suffering he saw a small vessel and was taken on board and found his way down south. He drew as best he could a rough map of the island and part of the bay, and wrote out some few particulars of the burying of a lot of treasure. The grandson of this oldest man found the paper, and after his father's death endeavored to interest some local people in the matter, so as to help him look up an island such as the one marked on the old faded paper. In some way Lynds heard of this paper and from some source got an outline of the old map, and found that Oak Island compared quite well to the rough sketch on the old paper."

This is a fanciful tale but there is little reason to give it any weight. It was probably concocted by treasure searchers to reinforce the contention that Kidd buried his treasure on Oak Island.

Most maps and charts seem to have been found in some old, dusty, and forgotten sea-chest tucked away behind a shroud of cobwebs in the corner of an attic or cellar. In a booklet written around 1917, entitled "The Lure of Pirate Gold," the late Josephine Fredea of Chester tells of an English map found in a an old oaken chest. Fredea writes:

"With the hope of securing such prizes to inflame their avarice, it is small wonder that a horde of lawless and adventurous spirits of many nationalities were soon sailing under the black flag. The last will and testament of one of these men has been recently discovered by a gentleman prominent in English literary circles.

"This gentleman, whose name I am not at liberty to disclose, recently purchased an old manor-house located near a certain seaport in England. Rambling over his new property he one day visited a long-unused room, where the dust lay thick on floor and furniture. His attention was attracted to an old oaken chest covered with quaint carvings. This he opened and discovered within clothing, nautical instruments, and a casket containing a considerable sum of money, several old maps or charts and other documents, as well as the last will and testament of the owner.

"The testator had evidently been a master mariner, presumably the principal in nefarious transactions, since his will began with a lengthy prayer for forgiveness for past misdeeds, the text of which left little doubt that on his death-bed his conscience was giving him serious trouble.

"Having done his best (on paper) to introduce himself favorably to the Great Judge before whom he was shortly to appear, he proceeded to bequeath to his son 'then on the high seas' all property and money of which he died possessed, including the casket of letters and diagrams containing instructions as to the location of certain hidden property.

"The significant fact that the old sea-chest had lain there undisturbed for so many years, since the clothing, nautical instruments and money were all of ancient date, induced the finder to sift the matter thoroughly. Investigation shows that about the year 1780 the testator's son was impressed from a merchant ship into the Navy and was killed in action. After further careful and exhaustive inquiry, the present owner came to the conclusion that the information was of great value and was about to embark on a search for the hidden property, when he chanced to read the story of Oak Island in *Collier's* magazine.

"He was immediately struck by its remarkable similarity to a certain island clearly indicated on the chart in his possession. Between this island, 'past Sesambre [now known as Sambro]' as it is written on the chart, and a certain islet in the West Indies, there is marked a clearly defined track; and although most of the writing thereon is in Spanish and Dutch, yet it is apparent at a glance that there was a well-travelled path between the two islands mentioned.

"Other papers showed that a removal and subsequent deposit of seven separate packages took place on certain dates, each package bearing separate symbols and initials.

"There is also a diagram of the Cove on Oak Island, in the form of a Dutch tobacco pipe, and to this diagram is attached a paper which has not been easy to decipher.

"Members of different companies engaged in excavation work on Oak Island, always believed that documents were in existence which would make plain the mystery of the Island, and the discovery of the old sea-chest shows that their opinion was correct.

"I am not at liberty to go more fully into a description of these documents, for reasons which must be at once apparent to you, but, when peace has at last been concluded and men once more take up the prosaic routine of daily life, some adventurous spirit will no doubt resume the search on Oak Island and finally solve for us its fascinating mystery."

The story loses some credibility by not disclosing the name of the gentleman who purchased the old manor-house and discovered the sea-chest and its contents. Still more credibility is lost by not going "more fully into a description" of the documents for reasons that the reader is presumed to understand. Also, one is left wondering what ever happened to the chart.

It seems reasonable to assume that old maps may have been used to actually search for a treasure on Oak Island. And, indeed, this apparently happened at least once. Around 1920, a story surfaced about a stranger named Captain Allen who appeared in Chester about 1880 or 1885 asking discreet questions referring to Oak Island. He spoke with a southern U.S. accent, wore a large white Stetson hat, was handsome, and well-dressed and appeared to have lots of money. In his book *The Oak Island Mystery*, Reginald V. Harris tells the following story about this stranger:

"He purchased a small sloop for $1,200 from a fisherman named Granter at Shad Bay, a nearby settlement. He had with him an old chart which he kept to himself, worded, it was said, in a foreign language believed to be either Swedish or Spanish, and which he examined frequently. With a crew of two fishermen, Zinck by name, from the village, he sailed out of the bay in the very early morning, heading for a position 30 miles off-shore, where he took the altitude of the sun. This location has been determined as 44° North, 63° West (the approximate latitude of Oak Island). Then, turning his vessel, he sailed towards the shore on a definite compass bearing towards the northwest. From time to time he checked his position on the old chart, always without aid from either of his crew. He kept up this procedure day after day during two successive summers, and then left the place as suddenly as he had come."

The course that Captain Allen always followed took him into St. Margaret's Bay rather than Mahone Bay so he never actually found the island.

After Captain Allen departed, a man by the name of Pickles from Halifax took over the search, using information that Allen had given him from the chart, but he too kept entering St. Margaret's Bay where no island of the description given to him existed. Then, one day he described details about the island he was searching for to a local fisherman by the name of Billy Ball who identified it as Cochran Island (then known as Redmond's Island) in Shad Bay. Pickles disclosed that the island he was looking for had three piles of stones and an old well on it. Cochran Island is about the same length and width as Oak Island. Pickles found three piles of stones, but no well—and no trace of a treasure.

It could well have been Oak Island that Captain Allen was searching for because three piles of stones were later discovered on the Island, forming the configuration of a triangle. And there is an old well nearby.

However, it seems odd that the island Billy Ball identified is in the very head of Shad Bay from which the searches departed. It is also peculiar that Captain Allen chose an insignificant inlet like Shad Bay (the bay is about four miles in length and roughly half way between

Chester and Halifax) as his home port rather than a more prominent one such as Halifax which is about the same distance as Shad Bay from the latitude and longitude named by Harris.

Even if a map or chart appears to be irrefutably genuine due to a sworn statement, its origins may still be questionable.

In 1931, a man by the name of James H. Smith and his father, John J. Smith of Roxbury, Massachusetts, were interviewed by Reginald V. Harris (previously mentioned) on the direction of Frederick Blair regarding an alleged treasure map of Oak Island. Both the father and son had once lived near Oak Island and Blair had learned that they claimed to have once seen a document pertaining to treasure buried on the Island.

James H. Smith made a declaration under oath regarding the document and both he and his aged father signed and swore to its truth before a notary public. James H. Smith's stated:

"When I was a boy living at home in Greenfield, County of Colchester, Province of Nova Scotia, in the Dominion of Canada, I frequently heard my father John J. Smith speak of a chart, memorandum, or paper, then in possession of his father, Amos Smith, who lived in Shaw's Cove, County of Halifax, in the said Province of Nova Scotia.

"It was said by my father, John J. Smith, that the said chart or memorandum had reference to the burial of a quantity of gold on an island in Chester Basin in the said Province of Nova Scotia, and that my grandfather, the said Amos Smith, who had been a pilot working in and out of Halifax harbour, claimed that the longitude and latitude in said memorandum was in the vicinity of the entrance to said Chester Basin, and that the island described in the said memorandum was Oak Island, located in the said basin.

"I heard so much talk about the chart or memorandum that as I became older I determined to see and examine it personally, and to that end I went to the home of my grandfather where I did see and examine the memorandum and did read and study its contents most carefully.

"According to the best of my recollection and belief, the said memorandum told of the burial of a quantity of gold on an island located near a definitely-stated longitude and latitude, the figures of which I do not now remember. It stated that the island was about one mile in length and about one-half mile in width, was similar to a bottle in shape, two coves at the northeast end forming the bottle neck; and the island was wooded with oak trees. The memorandum then stated that on a hill between the two coves, a pit was dug to a depth of 165 feet, near a large oak tree from a limb of which they hung a block and tackle; that a vault was constructed at the bottom of the pit, and the vault was walled with granite stone 18 inches thick, and that the inside was lined with two ply of lead one-half inch thick. The vault was filled with gold bars, each four feet long and four inches square, and it was then covered with granite slabs. Two tunnels were dug 45 feet below sea level at low tide, leading from the pit to the shore in opposite directions, and there was placed in each tunnel an iron gate arranged so as to stop the flow of water, but these gates were left open to permit the water to flow through.

"The memorandum was inadvertently destroyed with other old papers, the property of the said Amos Smith, after his decease."

Inquiries were made and a marine pilot by the name of Amos Smith was discovered in Nova Scotia but he worked out of St. Margaret's Bay and not Halifax Harbour. Blair and Harris suspected that the document that the Smiths had seen was one that had been prepared by Amos Smith or someone well acquainted with the Oak Island searches. Indeed, the document may have been the prospectus of an early treasure company.

All of the old maps have one thing in common—none are now available. If any ever existed, what happened to them? Many old bibles containing valuable birth, wedding, and death dates have been passed down for generations. Why not the Oak Island Maps?

FIFTEEN

The
Show
Goes On

In the years following Henry Bowdoin's unsuccessful attempt in 1909, many interested people approached Frederick Blair to advance their theories on how to solve the water problem and recover the vaults and casks that had been discovered by the early searchers.

Blair recognized some of these people as charlatans, interested only in pulling a scam, and avoided them. Others had solid ideas that seemed workable, but they lacked the necessary funds.

Blair was only interested in attracting someone who could afford to take a gamble. He also wanted a person or firm who would retain the services of a professional engineer. Blair, who moved to Calgary, Alberta, in 1912, took his search for a self-financed individual to the news media and this advertisement appeared in the *Journal of Commerce* of Boston on December 7, 1922:

Buried Treasure

Speculative venture, partly proven, requires $50,000 for half interest. If successful, will produce millions within one year; otherwise possible eighty per cent loss. Satisfactory credentials, proofs partially successful efforts, will prove good sporting proposition for party financially able to take chance. Full frank details at interview. 228 F. Journal of Commerce.

The editorial page carried an article with reference to the advertisement that was undoubtedly of considerable assistance to Blair. It reads as follows:

Can buried treasure lure wall street?

"Two hundred years ago the Welsh buccaneer, Sir Edward [Henry] Morgan, descended on the town of Panama and relieved its inhabitants of as much of their wealth as he could take away. Some years later, when he died Governor of Jamaica, a rich and respected gentleman, the treasure he took from the Spanish Main had disappeared.

"The rest of the world apparently has forgotten about this, but there is a man in New York now who says he is certain that this or some other treasure is buried 150 feet deep at a certain spot on Oak Island, near Nova Scotia. Oak Island is one of the 365 islands in the neighbourhood, which are not inhabited regularly. This man, a native of Nova Scotia, is here to 'find men with imagination enough to risk some funds in a venture based upon records he possesses, which he believes will conclusively prove that treasure exists at a spot of which he has secured control from the Canadian government.'

"The story goes back to 1795, when three partridge hunters on Oak Island discovered in the solitary wilderness a place which showed the work of man. To this spot there have come successive parties of treasure hunters, who have dug deeper and deeper, and have worked out a well-defined pit. After over one hundred years of digging, there has been brought out of this pit cement, timber, salt water, metal, and a piece of parchment about half a square inch in area. However the individual interested, whose announcement appears on the front page of this paper, declares he now knows just where the suspected treasure is situated and thinks he can prove he does to any individual interested."

The advertisement and editorial stirred up a little interest but it was not until 1931 that Blair found an investor with enough money to head a new expedition. That backer was Chappells Limited of Sydney, Nova

Sir Henry Morgan, a 17th century Welsh buccaneer, whose treasure from the Spanish Main disappeared.

Scotia, contractors and manufacturers. Significantly, one of the Company's owners was William Chappell who had formerly been a member of the board of management of Blair's Oak Island Treasure Company from 1895 to its demise in 1900.

William Chappell was joined in the project by his son Melbourne, his brother Renerick, and his nephew Claude Chappell. Frederick Blair joined the venture as an employee and lived on the Island during the Chappell exploration.

William Chappell had been in charge of the drill in 1897 when the piece of parchment was brought up and disclosed information to Blair that he had kept a secret for 31 uneventful years. He told Blair that he had noted traces of yellow metal or gold on the bit when the particle of parchment was recovered. He had been reluctant to say anything about his observation at the time because the traces of yellow were so very faint.

Mel Chappell, who was a member of the Engineering Institute of Canada, talked with mining engineers regarding the best method for recovering the cement chamber discovered by the 1897 drillers. He was advised that a good cribbed shaft would best serve the purpose. Consequently, he and his colleagues decided to sink a shaft down to the chamber while keeping the work dry with a 450 gallon-per-minute electric pump.

Since no work of any importance had been carried out for 22 years since Bowdoin had ripped out all the platforms and much of the cribbing in the Money Pit, it was difficult to decide where to dig. The Money Pit had caved in over the intervening years and nothing remained but the suggestion of its location. Grass and weeds covered the Money Pit and all the Chappells had to guide them was a depression in the ground and a vague memory of the Pit's whereabouts. A disagreement flared up between William Chappell and Blair as to the exact location of the original Pit. Blair claimed that Chappell had staked out a spot that was six feet from the true location.

Not being able to agree on the "exact" place, they compromised by putting down a relatively large shaft 12 feet wide by 14 feet long.

They laid an electrical underwater cable from the mainland to run the pump, and sank the new shaft 163 feet deep. Beyond that, they probed by drilling an additional 12 feet down to what felt like solid undisturbed clay. (All the way down the digging had been through disturbed soil.)

The project failed miserably. They didn't find a trace of the iron, cement, wood, soft metal, or metal in pieces encountered between 126 and 171 feet in the 1897 drilling operation. There wasn't even a hint of the cement vault that was supposed to be there.

The only logical conclusion was that the new Chappell shaft had been excavated in the wrong location!

But all was not lost. The diggers found a couple of possible artifacts. An old pointed part of an anchor, called a fluke, was found at the 120-foot level. (The fluke was lost after Blair's death in 1951.) They also found an axe head that closely resembled an old Acadian axe in the

Annapolis Royal Museum, believed to be 250 years old. This find may have sparked the idea that the Acadians were responsible for the works on Oak Island.

It is noteworthy to mention in passing that on the way down they found tools and timbers from depths exceeding those that had been reached by previous searchers. Blair was extremely puzzled by this, and remarked:

"From 116 feet 6 inches to 155 feet, the earth in over half of the shaft was much disturbed. How these articles reached a depth of from ten to seventeen feet lower than any searcher ever reached is a question that must be answered.

"These tools, I believe, belonged to searchers who worked there many years ago, and had fallen from a much higher level to where [they were] found. Both [the axe and a pick] were in a perpendicular position and in soft, disturbed, or filled-in ground."

Blair gave the following explanation as to why they didn't find any trace of a treasure:

"The question now is, where is the wood and treasure—metal in pieces—which dropped from 100 feet, the iron struck at 126 feet by drillers, the cement and wood drilled into between 153 and 157 feet, and the iron at 171 feet? It appears as if we had gone past them. They certainly must be somewhere in the near vicinity of our Pit.

"It has been the theory of many connected with previous expeditions, that there was an open chamber below the deposit at 100 feet, and that this deposit fell into the chamber when the Money Pit collapsed years ago. There was certainly an open space of some description under that deposit, otherwise the result of the collapse would never have been so great a drop, if any collapse had occurred.

"I am convinced that down to 150 feet at least, one end of your [our] pit was [is] over the edge of what was once an open chamber. Due to collapse of supports, etc., above, this chamber has been filled with broken ground or clay, through which the water being pumped passed. Tons and tons of clay have passed out with the water this summer, and the gravel and other solids keep settling down to solid bottom as the work progresses. The wall of this chamber, undermined possibly by the water, has broken down in the vicinity of our pit, and perhaps it is some of that wall we have taken out.

"This is my theory. We certainly have a vast treasure here, and it will possibly require as much work to recover it as we have already done."

In addition to their misfortunes at not finding any trace of treasure, the expedition experienced serious mishaps, including a close encounter with death. The foreman, George Stevenson, was almost buried alive in a tunnel that was excavated from the 157-foot level. The first of two excavated tunnels was driven for a distance of nine feet from the north wall of the shaft and then stopped and a second tunnel was started from the same level on the east wall. The intention was to circle to the north and join the first. The purpose was to explore the surrounding area. It was in the second tunnel that Stevenson was almost entombed. Before reaching the end of the first tunnel, the ceiling of the second tunnel suddenly began caving in and Stevenson barely escaped with his life. This narrow brush with death was accompanied by pit accidents in which two workmen suffered broken ribs. We are also told that one man was killed and another lost an eye in accidents unrelated to the dig. •

Bad weather plagued the project and the electrical system running the pump was damaged several times by storms, causing the pump to stop. One of these electrical failures could have had tragic consequences had someone been trapped down in the shaft at the time.

In addition to the work on the Chappell shaft, the crew attempted to plug the flood tunnel near the beach at Smith's Cove by drilling and dynamiting but, like those who had tried before them, they failed. The did, however, dig up some fibrous material that was analyzed by Halifax botanists and determined to be coconut fiber.

Chappell's group did make a significant find that would create a turmoil of activity a few years hence. Mel Chappell stumbled on a stone triangle that had been discovered by Captain Welling in 1897, shown to Frederick Blair, and promptly forgotten. It was situated below the Money Pit near the high water mark of the south shore. The triangle was not given any particular consideration since it was believed to have been placed by an earlier search party for some unknown reason.

Work was called to a halt on October 29th after six months of toil and an expenditure of approximately $40,000.

Although Chappell intended to continue the project the following year, he came up against a brick wall. Sophia Sellers, widow of Henry Sellers who owned the eastern end of the Island, died in the same year the project began. She was succeeded by 12 heirs who refused to renew

Blair's lease, which expired in the fall that year, of 1931. However, Blair still held the treasure trove rights.

In 1932 and 1933, two search parties endeavored to locate the lost deposit using Blair's treasure trove license and the permission of the Sellers heirs. (For some unknown reason, the Sellers heirs allowed others to dig.) They drilled several holes and left empty-handed.

Then, in 1935, a man appeared on the scene who would make substantial strides in piecing together parts of the Oak Island puzzle. His name was Gilbert D. Hedden of Chatham, New Jersey.

Gilbert Hedden became intrigued with Oak Island when he read an article in the May 8, 1928 edition of the *New York Times*. Fascinated by the engineering challenges, he began to contemplate applying his own talents and ingenuity.

Born in 1897, Hedden graduated from Newark N.J. Academy and took a two-year course at Rensselaer Polytechnic Institute. In 1919 he became Vice-President and General Manager of the Hedden Iron Construction Company, Hillside, New Jersey, a structural steel fabrication and erection company. The firm was sold to Bethlehem Steel Company in 1931 and Hedden was appointed plant manager of the "Hedden" works.

Hedden left the steel industry in 1932 and spent two years in the life insurance business. In 1934, he established an automobile dealership in Morristown, New Jersey, and he held the office of Mayor of Chatham from 1934 to 1938.

In view of his education and proven capabilities, Hedden was certain that he could solve the Oak Island riddle, where all others had failed. It was the challenge and no doubt the promise of adventure that attracted him. For men of Hedden's financial stature and business capabilities, the cash return on the retrieval of buried treasure is usually low on the list of motivators.

Hedden resolved to take on the Oak Island challenge and succeed where all others before him had failed. He signed an agreement with Blair in March 1935 and purchased the east end of Oak Island from the heirs of Sophia Sellers in July of that year for $5,000. (Excluding the treasure recovery potential, the land had a "rental value for pasturing" of only $15 per year.)

Hedden no doubt observed that there had been a lot of "do it yourselfers" involved in the Oak Island treasure hunt. (Frederick Blair and William Chappell appear to have done their own engineering except for bits of advice solicited from mining engineers.) Even Henry Bowdoin with his broad scope of engineering expertise had failed. Hedden decided to hire experts to recover whatever was at the bottom of the Money Pit. In April 1936, he signed a contract with Sprague and Henwood, Incorporated, of Scranton, Pennsylvania, who had participated in an earlier search. They were hired to de-water and reexcavate the Money Pit, the Chappell and other shafts, and conduct lateral drilling from depths between 125 and 160 feet.

Hedden was certain that the venture was destined to succeed because the firm was going to utilize the latest in modern technology and apply new methodology. Sprague and Henwood proposed to apply no less than a 1,000 gallon-per-minute pump, figuring that a machine with that capacity would certainly pump the Money Pit dry as a bone.

In addition to applying one of the most powerful pumps available, the firm proposed to locate the deposit by lateral drilling at two-foot vertical intervals with drills extending into the side of a shaft for a distance of 20 feet. How could Hedden fail?

The Sprague and Henwood crew opened and retimbered the Chappell shaft to a depth of 170 feet—the greatest depth ever reached up to that time—but found no trace of a treasure. Two wood splinters that they found at 150 feet were believed to have come from a chest or platform that had fallen in the 1861 collapse of the Money Pit. At this stage and in consideration of the lateness of the season, work was put on hold and resumed the following spring of 1937.

In order to give themselves lots of room to conduct the lateral drilling work, a new shaft (dubbed the Hedden shaft) was put down to a depth of 124 feet 6 inches. Adjacent to the Chappell shaft and twice its size, the shaft measured 12 feet by 24 feet. They encountered a band of clay resembling putty at 93 feet. It was different from any soil previously found. Far from treasure, Hedden used some of it to putty the windows of his shack on the Island.

They bored 15 holes vertically, each 42 feet deep, from the bottom of the new shaft. Oak varying from one inch to two feet six inches in thickness was bored through at depths between 148 and 157 feet. These

William S. Crooker

Remains of the Hedden Shaft; 1976 photo.

results indicated to them that they were hot on the buried treasure's trail, but financial problems halted the search.

Hedden had intended to resume work the following year but wrote Reginald V. Harris, Blair's lawyer, on March 25, 1938, that an expansion of his automobile business would be consuming all of his time and money indefinitely.

The expedition had cost Hedden over $50,000 and, unbeknownst to Blair, he was in financial trouble. The United States Internal Revenue Service was suing him for back taxes in connection with the 1931 sale of a steel-fabrication business. After years of litigation, Hedden almost went bankrupt. He was forced to sell most of his assets to pay taxes and almost lost the Oak Island property. But despite his financial problems and inability to resume work on Oak Island, his curiosity and interest remained and he made visits to the island as late as the year before he sold the property in 1950.

Hedden's most significant discovery was the oak borings that were brought up from below the bottom of his second shaft, which indicated the position of the lost deposit. But he conducted other work that threw light on what was to become one of the most enigmatic pieces of the Oak Island puzzle—the stone triangle Captain Welling had discovered in 1897.

SIXTEEN

The
Stone
Triangle

In June 1937 while Gilbert Hedden was conducting his search, Reginald V. Harris, lawyer for Frederick Blair and Hedden, picked up a book that had just been written, *Captain Kidd and His Skeleton Island* by Harold T. Wilkins of London, England. The book contained the map of an island which Harris noticed was similar in shape to Oak Island.

Harris showed the book to Hedden who studied the map at length. He noted several items of similarity, including shoreline configuration, offshore water depths and shoals, two mountains and a lagoon (corresponding to Oak Island's two hills and a swamp), and a cross mark in the vicinity of the Money Pit.

The map bore the legend W.K. 1669 with the following distances and bearings:

18 W and 7 E on Rock
30 SW 14 N Tree
7 by 8 by 4

The island on the map was unnamed and there was no designation of latitude and longitude. The water around the island was unnamed as well, showing only the words "Mar Del" (sea of?).

The author claimed that the map and three similar to it had been discovered in the secret compartments of three sea-chests and a desk, alleged to have once been owned by Captain William Kidd. Hubert Palmer, a British antique dealer of Eastbourne, Kent, had purchased the items in the early 1930s and shown the maps to Wilkins.

Hedden wrote to Wilkins pointing out the similarities between Oak Island and the island shown on the map and requested additional information. Wilkins replied that although the map was genuine there couldn't be any connection with Oak Island because he knew the latitude and longitude of the island in his book which placed it in a sea of the eastern hemisphere, far from the Atlantic Ocean. He further advised Hedden that Kidd had never been near Nova Scotia. In a second letter to Hedden, Wilkins prevailed upon Hedden not to waste his time making comparisons between Oak Island and Kidd's island, which lay on the other side of the world.

However, Hedden was not convinced. On discussing the matter with Blair, he learned of the stone triangle Captain Welling had discovered in 1897. Blair also told him that there was a white granite boulder with a hole drilled in it not far north of the Money Pit.

Hedden couldn't contain his curiosity. It was mid August 1937. Although digging in the Hedden shaft was well underway, he discontinued the dig to investigate. He and his men made a thorough search of the eastern end of the Island. There, they found the white granite boulder with the drill hole, about 50 feet north of the Money Pit. Then they found another one, unknown to Blair, near the shore of Smith's Cove and about 400 feet from the first. Both boulders were marked with drill holes two inches deep by one and a quarter inches in diameter which were obviously man-made.

Further searching quickly located the stone triangle near the south shore. Fred Nolan, who had investigated and photographed the triangle, (which was later destroyed by a search party in the mid 1960s) described it to me in an interview in 1975. He said that it had been situated about 50 feet from high water mark of the south shore and was composed of large granite beach stones about 12 or 14 inches in diameter. The stones were arranged to form a large equilateral triangle measuring about nine or ten feet on each side with the base of the triangle running approximately east and west. A median line of stones ran from the base to the apex in a true north direction beginning at a distance of four feet along the line of the base from the most westerly corner of the triangle. The significant feature of the triangle was that an extension of this line from the base to the apex intersected the supposed position of the Money Pit.

From other sources I learned that an arc of stones situated about three

Frederick G. Nolan

The stone triangle. Notice a chiselled cross mark on the rock near the bottom of the photo. This rock formed the apex of the triangle. The dark square object beside the tree is an attache case placed to give an idea of the size of stones. The triangle was destroyed in the mid 1960s as a result of excavation work on the shore.

119

feet below the triangle's base connected its east and west corners and that the median line crossed the base and extended down to this lower line of stones. The entire configuration is said to have resembled a giant sextant. Nolan told me that the curved line of stones below the base was obscure when he investigated the triangle.

Hedden now strongly suspected that the map's cryptic legend held an important clue and engaged a professional surveyor. On August 16, 1937, Charles Roper, a Nova Scotia Land Surveyor of Halifax, arrived with his young assistant, George Bates. On measuring the distance between the two drill holes, Roper and Bates found the distance to be 415 feet, or almost 25 rods. (One rod equals 16-½ feet.)

Applying the measurements given in the map legend, Hedden instructed Roper to establish a point on the line joining the drill holes in the rocks at 18 rods east of the rock north of the Money Pit and seven rods west of the rock near Smith's Cove. Roper laid off a point which fell close to the Cave-in-Pit! Hedden was intrigued with the results the survey was producing and instructed Roper to strike a course from this point in a southwest direction towards the south shore. He was astounded by what followed.

At a distance of 30 rods, Roper struck the median line of the stone triangle at a point just below the triangle's east-west base. Roper then discovered that the median line was on a true north bearing and its prolongation northerly passed across the Hedden shaft and struck the westerly drilled rock, north of the Money Pit.

The direction "14 N Tree" fell far short of the Money Pit which measured about 18 and not 14 rods from the apex of the triangle. Nothing at all could be construed from the "7 by 8 by 4" notation. Nevertheless, Hedden was certain that the cryptic legend on the map held important clues to the solution of the Oak Island riddle and decided that he must go to England and visit Wilkins.

Hedden boarded the *Aquitania* on November 10, 1937, and set sail for London. His interview with Wilkins is best described by the following quote from a letter Hedden wrote to Reginald V. Harris:

"Wilkins is a very peculiar character, and it is difficult to describe him adequately. I would say that in appearance and manner of speech he is every bit as crazy as his book would seem to make him.

"He almost immediately admitted that the chart as shown in the Kidd book is simply a figment of his imagination and apologized sincerely for

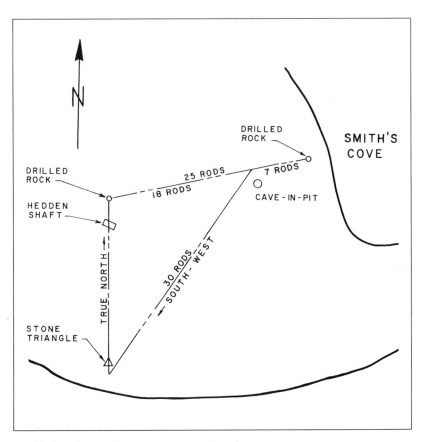

Drilled rocks in relation to stone triangle.

not being able to tell me before that it was. I am sure he is getting into a bit of hot water in that regard, as he has received many letters from all over the world in which the writer professes to identify the island and offers to give its location. He admitted my claims to identify far surpasses any others he had received and agreed that his drawing was according to the evidence undoubtedly of Oak Island. When he had submitted his book to the publishers, they demanded that he include some sort of map or chart. He put the request to Palmer [the antique dealer] who absolutely refused to permit any of the charts to be reproduced. Wilkins therefore drew the chart as shown, using symbols and marks shown on contemporary charts on file in the British Museum. The only actual marks [that he saw on Palmer's charts] were the

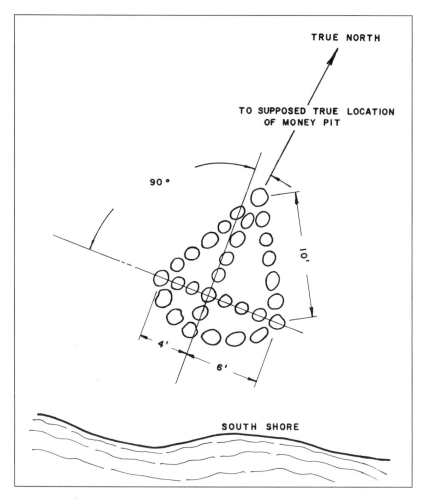

Diagram showing how the triangle could have been an indication of the treasure's location.

valley and the lagoon, and he unconsciously made the general shape somewhat the same as the actual Kidd charts. The legend of the directing measurements simply came out of his mind and had no basis in fact at all. Later just before the book was published, it was necessary to make a frontispiece and, not having the first drawing in his possession at the time, Wilkins reproduced it as well as he could from memory, which accounts for the difference between the chart in the book and the one on the front and last page.

"After I had convinced him that I had actually found markers at the points designated in his imaginary directions, he was amazed and went to great lengths to convince me that he had never been in America and had never seen an outline of Oak Island. As he became more and more convinced of the truth and sincerity of my story, Wilkins, and this may be a good commentary on his character and mental capacity, began to be convinced that he was a reincarnation of Kidd or some other pirate and had been selected to disclose the secrets of this long hidden hoard to the modern world. By the time I left, he was completely certain of it."

Accepting Wilkins' confession, one must ask, "Why did the markers found on Oak Island agree with the ones Wilkins had imagined?

I discussed the matter with Fred Nolan, who has done a lot of surveying on the Island, and he suggested that the drill holes in the rocks could quite possibly have been set by an early search party to reference the line of the flood tunnel from Smith's Cove to the Money Pit. Nolan and I concurred that the 415 feet which is two and a half feet off of 25 rods could be a pure coincidence. As for the "30 S W" given in the legend, Robert E. Restall, who headed an expedition in the early 1960s, suggested that the distance from Roper's point on the line between the drilled rocks, marked with a steel pin, to the base of the stone triangle was less than 30 rods. In a letter to Reginald V. Harris dated May 1, 1961, Restall said: "The diagonal line from the steel pin to the base of the triangle is 6' short of 30 Rds." Restall further stated that the Cave-in-Pit was two rods (33 feet) southeast of the steel pin which is not so "close" as one might expect. The problem with Restall's statements is that he was not a land surveyor and it is unknown if his data was provided by a Professional Surveyor or verified by one. In his letter, Restall refers to the steel pin as "put in by Hedden." He probably meant "by Roper" but there is the possibility that Hedden or someone else placed the steel pin after Roper finished his survey and may have planted it in the wrong location.

Nevertheless, there is no apparent reason why the map in Wilkins' book bore so many similarities to Oak Island. And furthermore, why was the median line of the stone triangle laid out in a true north direction? If it had been placed there only to reference the Money Pit, a true north orientation would have been unnecessary. To this day, it is unexplained.

SEVENTEEN

Tragedy Strikes

Wile Gilbert Hedden carried out his 1935 to 1937 search, Edwin H. Hamilton, Associate Professor of Engineering at New York University, was waiting in the wings to take the spotlight.

When Hedden was forced to drop out of the treasure hunt, due to financial problems, in the spring of 1938, Hamilton jumped in and offered to continue the search. Hedden, who still owned the land, and Blair welcomed his offer but dragged his feet when Hedden suggested that they split the take three ways. Blair had been accustomed to an entitlement of one-half and negotiations continued for a couple of months before an agreement was reached. Hamilton and Hedden would each take 30 percent and the balance of 40 percent would be given to Blair.

With the breakdown of "who gets what" completed, Hamilton entered into an official agreement and began work in the middle of July 1938, engaging Sprague and Henwood, who had worked for Hedden, to continue with the drilling operation.

Despite the outbreak of World War Two in September 1939, Hamilton carried out a two-phase operation for the next five summers at a cost of $58,000, employing as many as 14 men. One phase consisted of deepening the Hedden shaft and drilling into the sides in an attempt to locate the lost deposits. The other involved exploring, recribbing, and mapping many of the shafts and tunnels of previous expeditions.

In that first summer of 1938, 58 holes were bored laterally at various levels in the Hedden shaft. The drilling was carried out at various angles to the horizontal, producing fragments of very old oak from 119 feet deep and slightly north of the Chappell shaft. When consulted on these findings, Hedden said he thought that the oak was from the remains of the 1861 collapse of the Money Pit, seemingly pinpointing its location. The exact location of the Money Pit had been lost for many years but now that problem appeared to be solved.

The second phase of Hamilton's project ran concurrently with his work on the Hedden shaft. Considerable time and effort was spent exploring tunnels beneath the Island that had been dug by early search groups, but it contributed nothing towards solving the puzzle.

Turning to the Chappell shaft, Hamilton deepened it to 176 feet where he struck a 24-foot thick layer of limestone bedrock. He drilled down through the limestone to a depth below 200 feet and brought up chips of oak. Drilling probes by a later search group would suggest that the wood chips were part of a man-made structure.

Hamilton continued to investigate until the summer of 1943 when World War Two interrupted his expedition.

Hamilton didn't return to live out his life in New York but chose to stay, and he found a livelihood in Nova Scotia. He joined Amos Nauss, one of Hedden's former workers, in a boat building business at Marriott's Cove, near Chester, where he lived until he died in 1969.

Despite the trauma and strife of World War Two, Blair, Hedden, and their lawyer, Reginald V. Harris, continued to receive numerous inquiries about Oak Island. Harris writes in his book about the Island: "Some of these enquiries were made out of mere curiosity, some were to advance 'crackpot' theories; others were apparently serious in their desire to undertake the recovery of the treasure 'subject to certain conditions.' On one occasion a young man purchased for $125 a map, sold at a radio station in New York, and arrived by air a few days later, equipped with a pick and shovel to begin work! He did, in fact, go to

Oak Island, but after turning a sod or two, told the writer that he stood a better chance of getting a pair of nylon stockings in Halifax (where, at that time they were not procurable at all) than of recovering Captain Kidd's treasure on Oak Island! With such equipment he was probably right!" That attempt was the briefest ever made and took place in May 1946. The treasure hunter was a 26-year-old G.I. by the name of Nathan Lindenbaum who hailed from New York.

Around the same year that the G.I. arrived with pick and shovel, Anthony Belfiglio, an engineer from Toronto, tried to buy a piece of land containing the Money Pit from Hedden for $15,000. He said that he had backers who were prepared to put up $50,000 to launch a recovery project on the Island. Hedden told him that he would sell all his lots on the Island—not just the immediate area of the Money Pit— and the price would be $25,000, not $15,000. The deal fell through.

As it turns out, Hedden should have taken Belfiglio's offer because he ended up selling his Oak Island lots on May 12, 1950, for only $6,000. The purchaser was a 60-year-old New York mining engineer by the name of John Whitney Lewis, with 38 years experience as an engineer. His interest was kindled by a reference to Oak Island in the letters column of *Newsweek* magazine in January 1950, and he resolved to tackle the mystery.

Lewis purchased the property thinking that he would both own the land and hold a license to dig. It was his understanding that Blair's treasure trove license (a permit issued by the government giving right to search for "treasure trove" with five percent of the value of recovered treasure to be paid to the Province) had expired on June 30, 1949. It had, but Blair had previously applied for and received a new license on July 14, 1950, for a five-year period. Mel Chappell who had worked with his father William on Oak Island in 1931 had entered into a prior agreement with Blair to begin a new operation on the Island, leaving Lewis out in the cold. A conflict arose in which Blair wouldn't allow Lewis to dig and Lewis denied Blair access to the Island. But due to the enactment of a new Treasure Trove Act of that year, Blair applied for and was granted a special license that permitted him the right to trespass.

The new legislation permitted the holder of a treasure trove license to apply for a "special" license of trespass in a situation where the owner of the land denied the licensee permission to search. The license was conditional on the landowner being compensated for any damages to his property.

Lewis opposed the legislation but his appeal was denied. Discouraged by the impasse, Lewis sold the property to Mel Chappell. The transfer of land took place late in 1950. Then, on April 1, 1951, Frederick Blair died at the age of 83 and Mel Chappell took over Blair's treasure trove license. For the first time, the ownership of the land and the license to search on it was held by one person.

As soon as Mel Chappell acquired the Oak Island land, he pursued the treasure hunt with the help of a gold-finding machine that involved the application of photography.

Unknown to Chappell, the machine had been around for more than a decade. In 1936 Gilbert Hedden had been contacted by a man (name unknown) who claimed to own a gold detection device called a "Mineral Wave Ray" which had been invented by Welsford R. Parker of Windsor, Nova Scotia. When the machine's owner requested permission to bring it onto the Island, Hedden refused.

The following year, Hedden's attorney, Reginald V. Harris, ran into a fellow lawyer friend who had formerly represented the owner of the invention. Harris' legal friend had been given a demonstration in his office and he described what he had witnessed to Harris who in turn related the story in a letter to Hedden on October 21, 1937. Harris wrote:

"The lawyer hid 50 two-dollar bills in a law book on one of the shelves in his law office...and allowed [the demonstrator] to enter the room and take a photograph of the interior. [He] gave no indication where the money was deposited. He then changed the bills to the lower left-hand corner of his brief case lying on a chair, and again a second photograph was taken without any knowledge on [the demonstrator's] part as to where the money happened to be. These photographs were taken away and developed and later copies sent to [the lawyer] with rings around the law book and the lower left hand corner of the brief case, indicating where the money had been placed. The lawyer was amazed at the results and was converted to believe in the invention."

The owner of the machine kept pestering for permission to take it on the Island to locate the treasure. Finally, Hedden succumbed. In the summer of 1938 the owner's group arrived with the equipment but only stayed one day. They left saying that adjustments to the internal circuitry had to be made and Hedden wrote the machine off as a hoax.

Twelve years later, Mel Chappell heard about the Parker Contract Company of Bellville, Ontario, which reportedly was experiencing a degree of success with a mineral detection system based on photographic technology. Unaware of Hedden's experience with the machine, he arranged to have it incorporated in his search.

In December 1950 the "Mineral Wave Ray" was brought to the Island by its inventor, Parker. The machine consisted of a black box about two feet in length filled with radio tubes, resistors, wires, and batteries. A sample of whatever was being sought was put inside the box and a photograph of the area under investigation was placed in front of a camera lens-like protrusion at one end of the box. Parker located a spot about 150 feet from the Money Pit and told Mel Chappell that a large deposit of gold lay about 20 feet below the ground surface. Chappell barged a 20-ton steam shovel out to the Island and excavated a hole 30 feet in diameter and 50 feet deep, but no treasure was found. Parker located four other deposits and Chappell probed the locations with a drill but, again, nothing was found. These lame-brain explorations cost Chappell $35,000!

After the "Mineral Wave Ray" experience, Chappell was not prepared to throw any more of his own cash into the Money Pit so he decided to look for someone else to finance and head a search. His input would be a no-charge lease and the use of his treasure trove license in return for a one-half share of the take.

Chappell received numerous proposals but the first acceptable one was made in 1955 by George Greene of Corpus Christi, Texas, who represented five large oil companies. It now appeared that "money" would finally accomplish the task that had always been aborted by shortages of funds.

Greene, a burly cigar-chewing petroleum engineer complete with wide-brimmed Stetson and cowboy boots, did some research before commencing operations. He read the manuscript of *The Oak Island Mystery* by Reginald V. Harris, and delved into the Provincial Mines records and documents lodged at the Nova Scotia Archives. With lots of money behind him and an in-depth study of Oak Island under his belt, he confidently tackled the problem.

Greene's enthusiasm was kindled by the fact that his uncle, John W. Shields of Oklahoma City, had been associated with Franklin D.

The Halifax Herald Ltd.

George Greene (right), during his 1955 exploration of the Money Pit, examining a piece of drilling equipment with Cecil Lewis of New Glasgow, Nova Scotia.

Roosevelt during Bowdoin's expedition of 1909. Roosevelt's interest gave credence to the Oak Island story. "My principals have sent me up here to prove or disprove the legend, and if there's anything there we are going to find it," Greene said.

Greene's syndicate proposed to carry out a core drilling program all over the Money Pit site and locate the lost deposit. Greene said that this would be the first application of oil drilling methods on Oak Island in "the search for the gold," and that the Texas backers were willing to spend "any amount of money" if the drilling results were encouraging. He told newspaper reporters, "If we don't hit a concrete vault with this drilling we'll pack up and I'll head for South America and an oil-drilling job." In the event of failure, Greene advised the press that there was a strong possibility that Hollywood would want to make a movie about Oak Island. He said, "So if we don't find the treasure we may get our money back with the movie rights."

The oil men and Chappell signed a contract in September 1955 and the plan was put into action that fall.

Chappell showed Greene the 1897 drilling records, pointed out the approximate location of the Money Pit, and Greene began. He drilled four holes with a four-inch core drill in the Money Pit area and reported finding platforms every ten feet down to about the 112-foot level. "Below that there is nothing but cavity. The drills just drop right through. We went to 180 feet in one hole before we found the bottom of [the] cavity," Greene reported. He then pumped 100,000 gallons of water into the cavity to determine its size, but it disappeared leaving no clue as to where it went.

Greene left the Island in October with the intention of returning the following spring, but an oil drilling contract took him elsewhere and he never came back.

Nevertheless, Greene had made a significant contribution to the collective body of knowledge. This was the first time anyone had proven the existence of a cavern, natural or man-made, beneath the Money Pit.

George Greene was followed by two brothers from northern Ontario, William and Victor Harman.

William and Victor believed that the deposit consisted of gold buried by the Spanish during the conquest of the new world and they anticipated recovering as much as 200 million dollars. With this enormous return in mind, the brothers signed a one-year agreement with Mel Chappell and set about work in May 1958.

Using professional drillers, the Harmans reported bringing up fragments of oak, spruce, coconut fiber, and ships' caulking from depths of around 150 feet and greater in the vicinity of the Money Pit.

It is not known how much the brothers spent, but their money ran out after a couple of months of drilling and the Ontario Securities Commission refused their application to establish a public stock company unless they could obtain a five-year lease on Oak Island. Without knowing whether the brothers would be able to raise the required funds to continue the operation, Chappell refused to renew the lease.

Nevertheless, their findings were pertinent in that they supported Hedden's contention that the deposit was located 150 feet underground.

The next person who tried to match wits against the unknown engineer of the booby-trapped Money Pit was Robert Restall, a former daredevil motorcyclist.

Restall used to perform a breathtakingly dangerous act with his wife Mildred called the "Globe of Death," in which the two sped on motorcycles in opposite circular directions. The "Globe" was a 20-foot diameter steel mesh sphere in which Robert and Mildred travelled at speeds up to 65 miles per hour. Mildred rode around the sphere horizontally while Robert looped around the top and they passed each other within inches. The act was not accident-free. Mildred broke her jaw and Robert broke an arm at a performance in Germany.

After touring in circuses and carnivals throughout North America and Europe for 20 years, the Restalls finally gave up show business in the early 1950s and they settled down in Hamilton, Ontario, where Robert found a job in the steel industry. But they were not cut out for such a secure lifestyle.

Robert Restall became hooked on the treasure hunt in 1955, at the age of 49, when he visited Oak Island and met George Greene who told of all the problems related to the mystery. Resolved to some day conduct his own dig, Restall resigned himself to wait with anticipation while Greene, followed by the Harman brothers, conducted their searches. During that time, Restall made the necessary financial preparations. In addition to a little money of his own, the funding was to come from friends keen on sharing a king's ransom. After giving five percent of the treasure's value to the Nova Scotia government, the rest was to be divided three ways: half to Chappell, and one-half divided between himself and his backers.

Restall's opportunity arrived in October 1959 when the Harman brothers threw in the towel. He signed an agreement with Chappell and

The Halifax Herald Ltd.

Robert Restall descending into one of the shafts that he had recribbed near the Money Pit.

set up camp with his 18-year-old son, Robert Junior. Mildred joined them the following year with their younger son Rickey, who was nine.

The accommodations were primitive. The Restalls lived in two 16-foot by 16-foot one-room shacks in which they set up a dining table and installed bunks, a gas range, and an oil heater. There was no running water or indoor toilets and no telephone, and they lived without electricity for the first year.

Nevertheless, Robert Restall considered the sacrifice well worth the expected gain. He estimated the value of anticipated treasure at 30 million dollars based on the publicized inscription of the inscribed stone found in the Money Pit in 1803: "Forty feet below two million pounds are buried." He converted the value of two million pounds in the 1700s (apparently when he thought the original works on the Island were carried out) to the present-day value of the British pound, and then converted the sum to dollars.

Restall arrived on the Island with only his life savings of $8,500. With so little money he was unable to rent heavy excavation equipment and had to settle for a pick and shovel. So, Restall first concentrated his efforts on Smith's Cove where he and his son Robert Junior dug 65 holes two to six feet deep in search of the fan-shaped drains. They found sections of them plus layers of eel grass and coconut fiber ranging from 8 to 24 inches under the artificial beach.

Eventually, Restall raised $11,000 from his Ontario friends and in 1961 he purchased the large electric 1,000-gallon-per-minute pump from Hamilton, originally bought by Hedden. With the aid of the pump in keeping the water down, Restall explored and recribbed parts of the Hedden and Chappell shafts. He also did some tunneling between 100 and 120 feet but found nothing of interest.

By 1964, Restall had reconcentrated his efforts on Smith's Cove and began digging shafts between the Cave-in-Pit and the Money Pit in a determined effort to destroy the old flood-trap.

Restall's second shaft was down to 27 feet on August 17, 1965, and he had a gasoline-powered pump running on the surface which was keeping the water down to a depth of four feet at the bottom of the pit. The details are not clear but Restall was either leaning over and looking down into the pit or climbing down the ladder and suddenly he was laying immobile in the murky water at the bottom. His son Robert, shocked by what he saw, yelled for help and then scrambled down the ladder to help his father. A moment later, Karl Graeser, Restall's 38-year-old business partner, appeared on the scene. On looking down into the shaft, he saw Restall and his son lying unconscious at the bottom and rapidly climbed down to rescue them. He was immediately followed by worker Cyril Hiltz, age 16, of Martin's Point and both he and Graeser fell from the ladder before reaching the bottom. Another worker, Andy DeMont, quickly followed and also fell as he tried to climb downward.

Several tourists and a group of young students who were in the area at the time heard the cries for help and came running to the scene. Among them was a fireman by the name of Edward White of Buffalo, New York. Since the day was humid and a gas engine was running, White immediately suspected carbon monoxide fumes and took the proper precautions. He tied a rope around his waist and had others feed it out as he climbed down the ladder. Reaching the bottom, he harnessed a portion of the rope to DeMont who lay unconscious and then frantically groped around in the muddy water in search of others. Finding no one and on the verge of passing out, he and DeMont were hauled up and revived by artificial respiration.

The press initially blamed the accident on "a deadly accumulation of toxic marsh gas that filled the lower levels of the pit." But some of the people present said that the gas had a "definite stink to it" and it is more probable that the cause was carbon monoxide fumes from the pump's gasoline engine.

Firemen from Chester pumped the shaft dry and it was a grim day when the bodies of Robert Restall and his son Robert Junior, Karl Graeser, and Cyril Hiltz were brought to the surface.

EIGHTEEN

Nuking the Island

The opinion has been occasionally expressed by investigators of the Oak Island enigma that with enough money and today's equipment, it is possible to quite literally take the Island apart. One enthusiast recently said, "After the expertise we exhibited in the Gulf War, there isn't any question about not being able to get whatever's down there. Why...we could build a water-tight wall around the Island and simply lift it out. It would be like cutting the core out of an apple." Unfortunately, from an archaeological point of view, one man took a stride in that direction.

Immediately following the Restall tragedy, Robert R. Dunfield, an experienced petroleum geologist of Canoga Park, California, and a graduate of the University of California at Los Angeles (UCLA), took over the operation.

Dunfield, who first heard about Oak Island as a young boy in Denver, Colorado, harbored the opinion that the mystery could be solved with the application of heavy excavation equipment. He noticed

Restall and his son digging with a pick and shovel and was undoubtedly moved to the opposite extreme.

So, in the fall of 1965, at the age of 39, Dunfield made the necessary arrangements with Mel Chappell and put his concept into action. To make the project financially viable, he enlisted several wealthy California backers who included John Nethercutt of Beverley Hills and G.R. LePerle of Bakersfield. The expedition also included Daniel Blankenship of Miami, Florida, later to become one of the Island's current treasure hunters.

Dunfield described the project as "a problem in open-pit mining but with the added difficulty of seeping water. We can complete the excavation successfully, if we can dig it dry." He also stated his belief that treasure caches were buried at various elevations.

Dunfield gave considerable thought as to what might be required in heavy equipment and he decided on a 70-ton digging crane with a 90-foot boom from which hung a large excavating bucket. The machine was capable of digging a hole 200 feet deep and 100 feet in diameter. To keep the hole dry, he proposed a 110,000-gallon-per-hour pump.

The plan was to situate the digging crane on stable soil about 40 feet from the edge of the hole to be excavated, and to have a man held by a safety harness on a nylon rope stand on the opposite edge of the pit and direct the crane operator. All excavated soil was to be deposited in a sluice and screened by a water filtering system to separate out all rocks and any other objects such as artifacts and precious metals. The plan was to go to a depth of 180 feet, and deeper if anything of importance was recovered.

But before applying the big machine, Dunfield first barged two bulldozers out to the Island and proceeded to rip off a 12-foot-deep layer of the surface soil over the entire Money Pit area. This exposed the cribwork of several old shafts and what appeared to be the Money Pit itself, judging from its position in relation to the Hedden and Chappell shafts. He then attempted to block off the flood tunnel from Smith's Cove by pushing hundreds of tons of clay over the beach with his bulldozers. He may have succeeded, for although the water in the cove was muddied, the water pumped from the Hedden shaft remained clean.

Having apparently blocked the flood system connected with Smith's Cove, Dunfield turned to the south shore flood tunnel problem. But first he had to bring over the big digging crane. To accomplish that he

The Halifax Herald Ltd.

Treasure hunters Robert Dunfield (right) and Mel Chappell, meet at the Money Pit.

built a one-lane causeway across the straight separating the west end of the Island from the mainland. The causeway—about 600 feet in length—took only ten days to construct. Approximately 15,000 cubic yards of fill (common soil and rock) were trucked and dozed to build the fixed link. The causeway project was completed on October 17, 1965.

Dunfield moved the big crane down to the south shore and dug a trench about 20 feet deep and about 200 feet long, parallel to the shoreline. While excavating this huge trench, he struck a refilled eight-foot-diameter shaft. Since this shaft was not cribbed and there is no

The Halifax Herald Ltd.

Robert Dunfield's excavator, used in the '60s in the search for the second flood channel discovered in 1898 by the Oak Island Treasure Company.

record of it having been dug by an earlier search group, Dunfield concluded that it was part of the original project prior to 1795. He then removed the infill which extended 45 feet down, but found no trace of a flood tunnel.

It is significant to mention that the mysterious triangle of stones that had so intrigued Hedden in 1937 may have had some unknown relationship to the infilled shaft Dunfield discovered. Covered with moss and embedded in mud, the almost-hidden triangle lay just 25 feet to the north of the shaft.

Having exhausted a lot of energy and money on the search for the south shore flood tunnel, Dunfield turned to the Money Pit itself in November. With the huge equipment, he dug a hole nearly 140 feet deep by 100 feet in diameter and ripped out most of the old cribbing from earlier shafts and tunnels, leaving only the Hedden shaft basically undisturbed. Throughout the dig, the project was besieged by mechanical breakdowns and heavy rains. The sides of the big pit kept caving in during the storms and one day's work was cancelled out by another day or two of rain. Dunfield estimated that the project was costing $2,000 per day. At one point he said he would have to "call it quits" if they didn't find anything at the maximum obtainable depth of 198 feet.

After more than two months of sluggish digging, Dunfield refilled the huge hole to provide a solid soil platform from which a drilling operation could be conducted. He planned to reexcavate the big pit the following spring when the weather would hopefully be better and the ground drier. But the dig wasn't entirely fruitless. The sifted and screened soil from the hole yielded pieces of porcelain dishware thought to have been made sometime in the 1700s.

Working from the soil platform, Dunfield drilled a series of six-inch holes to almost 190 feet. In several of the holes, he encountered the cavity or cavern that Greene had discovered in 1955. The drill struck a 24-inch layer of limestone at depths between 140 and 142 feet before dropping through a 40-foot void to bedrock!

Having accomplished everything he could at the Money Pit, Dunfield turned to the Cave-in-Pit. It is not known what he intended to accomplish here. Perhaps he was simply searching in desperation, grabbing at straws like a general fighting a losing battle. With the big machinery at his disposal, he may have gone on "a wild goose chase" in the hope of finding anything, however small, that might have helped to solve the

The Cave-in-Pit, ten years after it was excavated by Robert Dunfield. All that remains is a water-filled hole about 100 feet wide. It was originally a circular shaft six to eight feet in diameter.

puzzle. He excavated the pit to a depth of 108 feet, scooping out old timbers at 68 feet and again at 100 feet which were probably part of the Oak Island Eldorado Company (also known as the Halifax Company) tunnels. Again, mechanical problems and heavy rains ended the work and the sides of the pit rapidly caved in. The Cave-in-Pit had become a gaping volcanic-shaped crater 100 feet wide and as many feet deep.

Bad luck and Mother Nature had conspired to keep the secret of the original Money Pit engineer. His subterranean puzzle remained unsolved after a savage assault by modern machinery. Dunfield had been badly beaten. He had entered the project with all the confidence in the world. He had been sure that he would win. But he had lost and in more ways than one. The project had cost him an estimated $131,000.

Drenched to the bone, Dunfield returned to California in April 1966 after calling a halt to the project. His lease with Chappell terminated in August of the same year.

Dunfield's heavy equipment approach to solving the mystery stirred up a hornet's nest of criticism in the Mahone Bay area and many Island observers were horrified by the devastation. Although the criticism of the local people and tourists may have been based on aesthetics, it has been said that the damage was archaeological. Certainly, a vast amount of "visual history" was lost.

It is not known if any damage was done to the original works prior to 1795, but one significant piece of the Oak Island puzzle was lost forever—the mysterious stone triangle! It slid into the south shore trench through rain storm erosion after Dunfield's departure.

NINETEEN

Treasure
Or Not?

I n the mid 1960s, theories began to surface indicating that the
original workings found on Oak Island may have an explanation
unrelated to the deposit of a treasure.

While many of these non-treasure suppositions are intriguing, they
do not detract from the mystery although they run contrary to the
perception of a treasure consisting of vaults filled with silver, gold and
precious jewels.

One of the most outstanding non-treasure theories was put forth by
the late George T. Bates, a Land Surveyor, of Halifax, Nova Scotia. As
well as being a professional surveyor, Bates was a historian of considerable knowledge and a renowned cartographer. He was also the young
assistant who worked with Charles Roper when the mysterious stone
triangle was surveyed in 1937.

Bates advanced his theory on who did what and why in 1972, as guest
speaker at a meeting of the Canadian Institute of Surveying and
Mapping, held at the Bedford Institute of Oceanography in Dartmouth,
Nova Scotia.

He began reviewing the history of pirate activity on the coast of Atlantic Canada. He told his audience that although freebooters plundered the treasure-laden Spanish galleons in the East and West Indies, their activities were not confined to the Spanish Main. In the 17th century, the seas from Brazil to Newfoundland were infested with blood-thirsty buccaneers. From about 1650 to 1750, many pirates abandoned the West Indies and sailed northward to plunder off the coast of Acadia and Cape Breton. Using Cape Ray and Harbour Grace in Newfoundland as their headquarters, the freebooters preyed on numerous ships en route to French Canada and the New England Colonies.

"The pirates would have required a place to repair their ships," Bates said, "and Oak Island in Mahone Bay offered an excellent location. It is more than 25 miles west of the shipping lane of ocean-going vessels and is well hidden by Big and Little Tancook Islands."

Bates theorized that the works found in 1795 and following years were the remains of an old pirate shipyard. He believed that a cofferdam encircled the beach at Smith's Cove and was equipped with a gate through which a ship in need of maintenance or repairs could be floated in at high tide. As soon as the ship was secured inside the enclosure, the gate was closed and another opened letting all of the water inside the dock drain down to a subterranean chamber below the Island. The Money Pit was a shaft supporting a long vertical pipe from the bottom of the chamber to the surface through which the water was pumped out by a windmill and when necessary, manpower. By the time work on the ship was completed, the chamber was pumped dry and ready for another refill to accommodate the next ship.

As for the artificial beach, Bates believed that the area between the dam and high tide had been lowered to a depth sufficient to accommodate the ship's draft. This, he explained, was why the beach had been excavated between low and high tides. As for all the coconut fiber, it was from the hulls of ships under repairs.

When work on the ship was completed, the gate was simply opened and the vessel floated back out at high tide. The second tunnel from the south shore was easily explained. Bates speculated that there were two dry docks, one on each side of the east end of the Island.

As pragmatic as Bates was, his theory is flawed. It just would not have made any sense to build two drydocks on the north and south sides of the Island because one sufficiently large to accommodate more than one ship would have involved far less work.

Perhaps the strongest argument against Bates' hypothesis is that if pirates wanted to repair a ship they needed only to sail up into the Bay of Fundy where tides in the Minas Basin rise as high as 50 feet and more. (Mean tides average 38 feet and spring tides 50 feet at Five Islands.) What better place could a pirate ask for than the Bay of Fundy to work on the hull of a ship? In the upper reaches of the Bay a ship could remain high and dry for almost 12 hours. The head of the Bay of Fundy offers the greatest careening grounds in the world.

In my first book on Oak Island, I speculated that perhaps an early civilization with an advanced technology may have buried something on Oak Island that they wanted to conceal forever. I am not ashamed to admit that the speculation is rather far-fetched. Nevertheless, it may have sparked the imagination of another author to develop a theory on a slightly different tangent.

In 1975, George Young of Queensland, Nova Scotia, author of a book entitled *Ancient People and Modern Ghosts,* was project manager of an engineering firm engaged in the installation of a sewage disposal system for the Western Shore Community on behalf of the Municipality of Chester. He was tasked with constructing a sewage pumping station for the Oak Island Inn on the mainland about 3,000 feet north of Oak Island. On October 28, Young was excavating a hole about 30 feet inland from shore when the machine operator struck what he thought was bedrock, only seven feet below the surface of the ground. But to Young's astonishment, a hard thump with the machine's heavy excavating bucket produced an unexpected result. Young says, "The world is full of surprises and this is one of them; for, as the bucket struck the hard layer, it broke through, making a neat hole about three feet in diameter. It was as though we had made a hole in the top of an egg."

Young and his workmen could see water about six feet below the broken shell and they were amazed to discover a cavern 52 feet deep when they lowered an old car transmission down to measure the depth. But their surprise wasn't over. The water started to rapidly rise in the cavern and by the following morning had filled the hole above the surface of the shell to grade and was gurgling in a fast-flowing stream to the sea. They set up two large pumps and the water was lowered to a depth of six feet below the ceiling of the cavern. Gary Weisner, a young member of the crew, was lowered down into the hole and Young recorded his observations.

"With his back towards the sea, the roof curved behind him until it became vertical approximately four feet from him. To his right and left the walls curved downwards in a similar nature about four feet on either side, making the cavern about nine and a half feet wide at this point. The walls seemed to widen in an arc, so that they faded from his lighted vision, and in his estimation extended more than 30 feet below the hillside!"

Young advanced the following intriguing speculation.

Commercially related Atlantic crossings by peoples of the Mediterranean were common by 400 B.C. and the voyagers established numerous trading settlements along the Atlantic coast. The relationship with the native people was undoubtedly friendly and mutually beneficial as manufactured articles such as tools were traded for furs, leather, canoes, and unique handicrafts.

In those days, the water levels of the tides in Mahone Bay had been about 33 feet lower, exposing numerous limestone caves. About this time, a colony of Mediterranean people from the shores of Libya who were a mixture of Phoenician (Lebanese) and Greek stock are believed to have renovated and occupied these caves as living quarters. Improvements were made to their dwellings over the years. They joined separate caverns with tunnels and excavated shafts to ventilate their cavern habitats. Young writes, "As their numbers and years of occupation lengthened, many improvements were made to their dwelling places. Tunnels were excavated to join the separate caverns, and shafts dug from the surface to ventilate the underground systems. One very large shaft was dug through the heavy grey clay in order to ventilate a cavern at its base of rather gigantic proportions."

Life carried on in harmony with the native people for about 150 years and then around 260 B.C., trading vessels from the homeland stopped arriving because of the huge and atrocious first Punic war instigated by the ambitious and expanding Roman Empire. (By the time the war had ended in 238 B.C., Carthage had lost over 350 very large ships.) The colony in the new world eventually fell apart as its people assimilated into the "mode of life of their in-laws, the Micmacs," and the origin and identity of these early settlers was forever lost.

The next temporary settlers arrived around 470 A.D. They were groups of people fleeing vandals from Asia Minor and the Orient. Among these peoples were the Copts, an Egyptian-Arab sect who were one of the first to adopt the Christian religion. The Copts and others may have inhabited the caves and tunnels that had been built by the original visitors but they eventually vanished, probably acculturating with the native people as had their predecessors.

As Young's theory goes, around 1384 A.D., a large party arrived in Mahone Bay with something to hide which was of exceptional value to them and they found the old living quarters on Oak Island an excellent place for concealment. They built an oak platform across the ventilation shaft above the cavern (the tides were eight feet lower than today) and placed their valuables upon it. They then roofed everything over with another tier of logs to form a vault. They then constructed log platforms every ten feet to the surface to support the weight of each interval of back-filled soil. Side tunnels leading to the cavern were in-filled with stones from the beaches to make the chamber or vault inaccessible.

Young further speculates that it may have been the intention to never reopen the vault as they may have been "interring one of exalted rank," which explains the booby-trapped artificial beach and flood tunnel.

Another theory suggests that the chamber below the bottom of the Money Pit may be a "time capsule" containing a "treasure," but not necessarily one that falls within the strict definition of a treasure cache from the likes of a Spanish galleon.

This theory comes from the "Bacon-wrote-Shakespeare" believers, who say that Shakespeare couldn't have written the works to which he is accredited because he lacked the education, wisdom, and wit. They also claim that the plays and sonnets displayed a knowledge of law, medicine, and science that he could not have possessed. This belief is supported by the fact that William Shakespeare (1564–1616) was not a man with an impressive "formal" education. He quit school at the age of 13 to work as a butcher's apprentice and went on from there to become a stage actor of no particular fame.

On the other hand, Francis Bacon (1561–1626) possessed all the qualities that Shakespeare is said to have lacked. Bacon's books and essays display the same scope of knowledge and talent as those attributed to Shakespeare.

Francis Bacon (1561–1626), who some believed wrote the works of Shakespeare, Burton, Marlowe, and Spenser. Original manuscripts have never been found.

William Shakespeare

Robert Burton   *Edmund Spenser*

The Elizabethan court often scorned poetry and the theatre so it was not unusual for people of noble rank and high social status to protect their station in life by writing under a pseudonym or borrowing the use of a name from an existing writer or author. Bacon had a reputation to protect. He was appointed Solicitor General of the British Crown in 1607 and Lord Chancellor and Keeper of the Great Seal a decade later, so it is conjectured that he bought or borrowed Shakespeare's name. Furthermore, Bacon is also credited with the works of others such as Robert Burton, Christopher Marlowe, and Edmund Spenser.

The manuscripts of Shakespeare and the other three prominent writers have never been found and some have speculated (probably because of the tiny piece of parchment recovered from the Money Pit in 1897) that they lay in a vault beneath Oak Island. To the Baconian speculators, it seems more than a coincidence that so many manuscripts by various people from the same time period have seemingly vanished from the face of the earth.

Beacon's reason for preserving his original works is thought to be ego-related. The theorists say that he wanted the world to one day (perhaps hundreds of years later) recognize him as the author, and to know that he, almost single-handedly, was responsible for the renaissance of literature and philosophy we call the "Golden Age of Elizabethan Literature."

Dr. Burrell F. Ruth, professor of chemical engineering at Iowa State University of Ames, Iowa, wrote Gilbert Hedden a long letter outlining his theory of why Oak Island holds the original manuscripts credited to Shakespeare and others. Ruth wrote the letter shortly after he had read an article on Oak Island in the October 14, 1939 issue of the *Saturday Evening Post*. Ruth believed that the literary cache was probably protected in a vault immersed in tons of mercury. Hedden replied that one of the mysterious legends of local folklore claims that the Money Pit contains mercury. He told Ruth that he had never found anything to support that belief but he said that "one point in favour of your theory is that there does exist an old dump on the island in which are the remains of thousands of broken pottery flasks. That this dump is very old is supported by the fact that we found nearby an old coin and an ivory boatswain's whistle which experts tell us date back to the Elizabethan period."

Of course Ruth's theory was strongly influenced by the fact that a piece of parchment had been brought up from the bottom of the Money Pit but the hypothesis has something going for it, considering the effectiveness of the booby trap. It appears that someone may have planned to conceal something for a very long time. Perhaps, it was argued by proponents of the theory, if it was Bacon who engineered the Oak Island works, he envisaged a time when the world would possess the engineering capabilities to retrieve his literary treasure.

Finally, there are those who say that there is no mystery and the early stories concerning the discoveries stem from the over-active imaginations of men who mistook a natural phenomenon or accident of nature for a place of buried treasure.

The best-enjoyed fluke of nature theory is that the Money Pit was a sinkhole, the limestone formation beneath the Island serving as supporting evidence. An article in the defunct *Atlantic Advocate* magazine of October 1965 is an excellent example of the sinkhole supposition. A portion is reproduced in my *Oak Island Quest* book and reads:

"After visiting Oak Island and studying its history I suspect that the whole mystery is due to a natural phenomenon; that the legendary treasure is non-existent and the mysterious people who were supposed to have buried it merely a figment of the imagination and I do not believe that there is any evidence of human workmanship on Oak Island, prior, that is, to 1795.

"There is, however, plenty of evidence to show that an agency other than man has been at work on Oak Island: namely the wind, the sea, and an age-old upheaval of the earth's crust.

"The south coast of Nova Scotia is extensively faulted. Many deep fissures running inland from the sea are common in that area. There is strong evidence of such a fault on Oak Island, extending along the artificial beach, the tunnel, and directly through the 'money pit'. Over many thousands of years debris, washed in by high tides and heavy seas, could have accumulated in this fault until it has completely filled it up.

"I believe that what the original discoverers found when they landed on Oak Island in 1795 was not a treasure site, but only a sinkhole caused by slumping in the debris in the fault. Several feet wide, this filling would be softer than the surrounding ground, and give the impression that it had been dug up before.

"As the treasure hunters dug down and found layers of logs, tropical fibers and cement, they assumed that these had been put there by man. Yet the logs were roughly laid with out fastenings of any kind. Storms and high tides, and fluctuations in the sea level relative to the land which took place from time to time over the years could have forced the logs into the fissure and arranged them roughly in layers.

"The tropical fiber could have come from the Gulf Stream which passes very near Nova Scotia. Strong gales could have blown the fiber onto the shore, where it would have become trapped in the fissure in the same way as the logs.

"The cement, considered one of the most important clues, was probably a natural cement. This can be formed in the ideal conditions within a fault. Clay and angular pieces of stone can be bonded by a natural cementing agent such as iron oxide, which forms a breccia almost impossible to distinguish from cement. That found in the pit was sent to a laboratory for analysis, and the report that came back stated only that it resembled man-made cement."

The sinkhole theory is interesting but it is difficult to accept that the workings discovered on Oak Island are a natural phenomenon. Accidents of nature are common but there is a limit to how many can be credited to any one particular site. To explain all of the discoveries on the basis of "fluke" stretches the theory beyond credibility and renders it untenable. For example, the theory does not account for the tier of flagstones not indigenous to the Island; pick marks on the walls of the old original Money Pit; platforms with the log ends securely fastened into the hard stiff clay of the old original shaft; the mysterious inscribed stone found deep down in the Pit; saltwater flooding the Money Pit from a depth of about 100 feet in an area where the surrounding soil was hard clay, devoid of saltwater; the artificial beach with its tons of coconut fiber and fan-shaped rock drains; and the positive results of the 1849 drilling program which struck wood and pieces of metal, as well as the discoveries of subsequent drilling probes.

The freak of nature premise becomes far-fetched when applied to the coconut fiber found on Smith's Cove and in the Money Pit. The Gulf Stream swings easterly away from the coast of Nova Scotia at a distance of about 400 miles. It would have been an exceptional coincidence, indeed, if tons of coconut fiber had blown into Mahone Bay from the Gulf Stream and washed only onto the beach at Smith's Cove! There has been no record of coconut fiber being found on any of the other islands of the Bay or anywhere else on the coasts of Atlantic Canada except Sable Island, where hundreds of ships have been wrecked over the centuries.

Oak Island treasure believers far outnumber the skeptics. And, of all those who believe in the existence of an *enormous* treasure, perhaps no one is more convinced than Frederick G. Nolan, a current treasure hunter who owns the center portion of the Island.

Nolan contends that the booby-trapped Money Pit is only part of the puzzle and that the remaining pieces lie on his land near the center of the Island, where he believes most if not all of the huge treasure is concealed. He may be right but the Money Pit has been the site of many discoveries for nearly two centuries, and its present-day owners, Triton Alliance, hold to their contention that something of enormous value lies deep below the Island in the vicinity of the Pit.

Today, on the belief that a project of such a stupendous scope must conceal something of enormous material or archaeological value, parallel treasure hunts are underway. In 1992, the year of the writing of this book, Triton Alliance is exploring the Money Pit area while Nolan independently explores his quarter portion of the Island adjacent to the Pit. Some of their discoveries are most astounding.

TWENTY

A Parallel Search

F rederick G. Nolan first became particularly interested in Oak
Island in 1958 after reading Reginald V. Harris' book, *The Oak
Island Mystery*. Although he had previously heard stories about
the treasure hunt and had visited the Island, the book sparked his
curiosity and zeal for adventure. Nolan paid Harris several visits since
their offices were only a few blocks apart and he became determined to
take a turn at trying to fit together the pieces of the puzzle.

But there was a line-up. In 1958, when Nolan became interested, the
Harman brothers were exercising their one-year lease with Mel Chappell,
and Robert Restall was scheduled to move in immediately after it
expired. So, although Nolan was ready to launch his own attack on the
Money Pit, he was obliged to wait backstage.

But Nolan didn't stand idly by. "The clues, the marking system
given, and the survey of Charles Roper seemed to indicate there was
more to the picture than the Money Pit," he recalls. So he visited
Chappell and requested permission to conduct a survey of the Island.

Chappell saw no reason to object and gave Nolan the go-ahead. Nolan says his chief objective was to tie in (locate positioning by survey) everything that could be lost as a result of Chappell's drag lining (excavating by a machine dragging a digging bucket) around the Money Pit area. Chappell told Nolan that he was going to work with a chap named Wheeler from West Virginia who wanted to transport a large dragline (excavating machine) from South America. Wheeler never showed up but Robert Dunfield took over the search immediately following the 1965 Restall tragedy, and he did what Wheeler had proposed.

Accordingly, between 1961–1962, Nolan spent several thousand dollars on men and equipment in addition to losing a substantial amount of time from his survey practice to lay out a grid over the entire Island, referencing all relevant markers. It was a large project for a speculative venture, and, as such, exhibited Nolan's optimism. Dozens of lines, some thousands of feet long, were cut through brush and heavily wooded areas and 23 concrete survey monuments were established, complete with numbered bronze disks for accurate positioning of a transit or theodolite! Concrete and form-work materials for the monuments had to be brought over from the mainland by boat and the holes for the monuments were dug by hand. It was a thorough and labor-intensive survey and, significantly, objects that would later be lost (such as the mysterious stone triangle) were referenced to the grid.

On completing his survey, Nolan was convinced that an enormous treasure was waiting for the right person and he approached Chappell with an offer to take over the lease; he even suggested buying the Island. But Chappell refused since he currently had a contract with Robert Restall. Besides, he was interested in a wealthy individual or syndicate eventually taking over the dig. In desperation, Nolan contemplated the remote possibility that Chappell's title to the Island might be flawed so he visited the Registry of Deeds in Chester. He was acting on a hunch and it paid off. He discovered that Lot 5 and Lots 9 to 14 inclusive, comprising about a quarter of the Island, had never been conveyed to Chappell by transfer down from the original owners of 1935. Nolan told me, "I went to Chappell and tried to make arrangements to dig and he told me to 'go to hell!' That's when I checked into the records and discovered that he didn't own all the land he thought he did." The rest was easy. Nolan simply approached the remaining heirs of Sophia

Sellers and acquired the land for a price of $2,500 which he says was $700 more than the $1,800 Chappell had given the Beamish family in 1961 for one-third of the Island.

In April 1963, Nolan again approached Chappell and offered to trade his newly acquired lots for an opportunity to try his luck at the Money Pit. But as before, Chappell refused.

Nolan felt defeated. He had spent a small fortune in time and money on the survey, and had nothing to show for it. But his curiosity kept him busy studying his survey notes and preparing a map of all the collected data. And as he worked, it gradually began to dawn upon him that there was more to the mystery than the Money Pit and its flood system.

The three piles of stones that Captain Allan may have been searching for in the 1880s formed the corners of a triangle in the shape of an arrow head. They were situated on top of the hill just outside the eastern boundary of his property. The sides of the triangle were about 150 feet long and the base about 100 feet. Nolan said that the stone piles (one has since been destroyed) had diameters of about 12 feet and heights of about five feet and had always been considered an old observation place. The arrow-like formation pointed directly towards the center of the swamp on Nolan's property. When Nolan found these stone piles, he also found two large ring bolts set in granite boulders that were on his property. He drew lines through the stone piles and ring bolts and decided to excavate shafts where the lines intersected, expecting that one of these intersection points would mark the location of a treasure. Utilizing a six-man work crew, he dug two 30-foot-deep shafts in 1963–1964. Nothing was found other than an old two-inch brass buckle from the bottom of one of the shafts. "But where did it come from?" Nolan asks. "Perhaps time will tell."

Nolan had for some time suspected that there might be a watertight vault somewhere else on the Island with a shaft running downward. It was now time to test out this theory and he embarked on an intensive search of his lands. In 1969, he even drained the swamp. He was surprised by what he found. His property, which extends entirely across the Island on the east side, contained numerous markers and objects which he believes are related to the original works.

Nolan discovered rocks with round holes bored or chiseled into them and some had pieces of metal inserted into the surfaces. He dug up pieces of old hand-cut wood which he believes are from an ancient treasure chest (one piece has old iron hinges intact). He also found beach stones, bits of old wood, and metal beneath the swamp, and pieces of wood and rocks that Nolan believes are survey monuments associated with the Island's puzzle.

One of the most noteworthy discoveries that Nolan made public at the time was what he believes to be an old stone surveyor's monument which he describes as being "similar to the type used by surveyors today." Nolan verified that the stone was man-made by having it examined and analyzed by a geologist, Robert Grantham, who reported that, "The upper six or seven inches of rock have been exposed to the weather for quite some time. There were lichens growing on the upper four inches and below that are marks made by vegetation growth in the soil which surrounded the rock." He also reported that, "The rock was found on end. This is not a natural stable resting position for a rock of this shape." The monument is of sandstone. It is square in cross section with two sides smooth or natural and the other two sides rough as if cut by a chisel. Burn marks are visible suggesting that heat was applied to cut the rock. Nolan says, "Some have said that when placed on its side it resembles a Spanish galleon."

Nolan believes that the monument was definitely planted as a survey marker, bearing no relationship to a property boundary. It was found purely by accident while tracing a prolongation of the median line of the arrow-shaped triangle formed by the stone mounds. "I was crawling along on my hands and knees following this line with a hand compass when the compass actually bumped into it. That's when I found the pointed end of this stone sticking out of the ground," he recalls.

Nolan claims that numerous other rock markers have assisted him in his search, and that many are of sandstone. He told me that some of the sandstone objects had "marks and figures on them," adding that all of the rocks found in a "natural" state were granite, whereas the sandstones fitted into a pattern "placed there by others." Nolan concluded that the sandstones are not indigenous to the Island, but that they were brought there for survey purposes.

In 1971, Nolan was granted a treasure trove license and began digging. In 1973 he dug his largest hole about 650 feet northwest of the Money Pit. He picked the position from the intersection of lines projected from some of the previously found markers. But he found nothing and abandoned the hole after reaching a depth of 35 feet. "I was

Hole chiselled into granite boulder found on Nolan's property. Nolan thinks rock is a marker in a survey system associated with a treasure deposit.

Sandstone found by Nolan is thought to be an old survey marker. It was found in an upright position with the upper portion exposed.

exuberant when I started," Nolan recounts. "I dug a shaft where I thought the treasure was buried. I was just like everybody else who's tried to work on the Island. I thought I had all the answers but the Island has a way of humbling a man."

Nolan referenced all his findings to monuments on his grid system and began drawing lines through certain points and extrapolating them in search of mathematical relationships. Frequently, when he would cut and run a line between two previously discovered markers, he would prolong that line and discover another. A configuration was beginning to form and he knew that he was on to something big. But he ran into difficulty analyzing the maze of lines in an attempt to find a meaningful answer to what they represented. And, as he was working on this technical problem, he was confronted with another.

While Nolan was surveying and searching on his middle section of the Island, others continued to explore at the east end. In January 1983, the current Money Pit treasure hunter, Triton Alliance, launched a lawsuit against him. David Tobias, president of Triton, who had acquired Mel Chappell's land in June 1977, initiated a civil suit over title to the seven lots he had acquired from the heirs of Sophia Sellers including access across Crandall's Point. Tobias' suit also cited interference with tourism and the removal and destruction of artifacts.

The suit was born partly out of events that began 18 years earlier when Robert Dunfield built the causeway from Crandall's Point on the mainland to the western end of the Island. An armed guard was posted at the entrance to prevent Nolan from using it. "Dunfield himself used to sit out there with a rifle and threaten to shoot me if I tried to cross his causeway," Nolan told me, "He was Mister Macho Man."

Nolan retaliated the following year (1966) by purchasing land at Crandall's Point that abutted the entrance to the causeway. He then barricaded it. This created a stalemate which was temporarily solved in 1968 by a six-month agreement in which Dan Blankenship, who had taken over the operation on the Money Pit from Dunfield, paid Nolan $1,000 to cross the Crandall's Point land. When the agreement was later revised, Nolan acquired a few shares in the Money Pit operation in return for surveying on drilling work and granting Blankenship and his new partner David Tobias a right-of-way over his property. But the agreement was short-lived. It was annulled in 1969 when Triton Alliance was formed. Each side accused the other of breach of contract.

Nolan then again blocked off the causeway entrance, forcing Triton to construct a bypass road to it. In retaliation, Triton chained off the causeway where it meets the Island which was on Chappell's land, thus preventing Nolan access to his property in the center of the Island.

Now, Nolan was forced to take a boat from Crandall's Point to Joudrey's Cove where his property fronts on a section of beach on the north side of the Island. As a counter move, Nolan chained off the long-used and well-developed trail to the eastern end of the Island that crossed his property, thereby preventing Triton road access to the Money Pit. "Things got really heated up at this point," Nolan told me. "Dan came out one day with a rifle and it was rather frightening. The R.C.M.P. were called in before something terrible happened and they asked Dan what he was doing with the gun and he told them he had it to protect his property but they didn't believe him and confiscated it."

With no way to drive out to the Money Pit, Triton eventually built its own road which took a detour around Nolan's land.

Since the limitations of access were grossly inconvenient for Nolan, the parties eventually came to terms. Both parties signed an agreement in November 1971 stipulating that they would share information about their treasure searching, that Triton would receive 40 percent of any treasure recovered on Nolan's land and, most important for Nolan, that he would no longer need to take a boat to access his property. The agreement also provided Triton with its original access to the causeway but it precluded any legal action over title to Nolan's lots during the term of contract.

Throughout the 1970s Nolan plodded away on his treasure hunt, exhibiting his artifacts in a museum on Crandall's Point which he constructed in 1967, Canada's Centennial Year. But trouble flared up in 1974 when the Department of Transportation and Communication built a wider bypass road to the causeway. (The Department of Tourism had been paying Nolan a percentage of the revenue from the tours that it operated in exchange for passing over his Crandall's Point land.) Nolan contended that the new road had been constructed on his property and he lengthened his museum across the road in protest. As a result of Nolan's move, the Department of Tourism got out of the Oak Island tour business and turned its operation over to Triton.

The agreement between Triton and Nolan terminated with a lawsuit that was launched in March 1983. The research, discoveries, and trial proceedings ended in December 1985 with Triton losing its case with respect to Nolan's title to the seven lots. However, Nolan was ordered to compensate Triton with $15,000 for interfering with its tourist business and told to remove any barrier to the causeway, which included the portion of his museum he had built over the roadway. Triton appealed the court's decision only to again be denied its land ownership claim in November 1987. Also, Nolan had filed a cross-appeal regarding the ruling of damages and access across Crandall's Point and the Court reduced damages for lost tourism business to only $500 from $15,000. However, Nolan was ordered to remove the portion of his museum blocking the access road.

The civil suit finally ended at a cost of about $100,000 each, and life returned to normal on the Island. Nolan practices land surveying for a living, continues to access his property by water, study his discoveries and search for additional evidence and artifacts while Triton continues its operation at the Money Pit. But the relationship between Nolan and Triton is strained, and will probably remain that way.

Daniel Blankenship first learned of the treasure hunt while reading the January 1965 issue of *Readers Digest*. Between the covers was a story by David MacDonald, condensed from *The Rotarian* magazine. The article carried the title "Oak Island's Mysterious 'Money Pit'," and above the title there was an enticing statement, "There is *something* down there—but for 170 years no one has been able to solve the riddle of how to get at it."

Like Fred Nolan of seven years earlier, Blankenship also became "hooked."

In 1965, Dan Blankenship was a successful building contractor in Miami, Florida. Today, in his late 60s, he might be retired and basking in the sun with his wife Jeanie on a warm southern beach had it not been for that particular magazine story that he read at his kitchen table in Miami.

Twenty-seven years later, on January 15, 1992, I sat across from Dan at his kitchen table but it wasn't in Miami. It was in a bungalow on Oak Island overlooking the narrow reach of water that separates it from the mainland.

As we chatted, Jeanie stood at a nearby countertop working on the assembly of an intricate picture puzzle, containing thousands of tiny pieces. "It isn't all that hard," she explained, "it just takes a lot of concentration, time, and patience," and she showed me a beautiful project she had completed laying nearby on the floor.

Meanwhile, Dan is working on another sort of puzzle. It's a puzzle that motivated him to give up a successful contracting business, sell their Miami home, and start a new life in Nova Scotia.

But it didn't all happen in one fell swoop. Blankenship first began by visiting the Island in the summer of 1965 where he met Restall and Dunfield. He was so impressed and intrigued by the mystery and what was being done that he invested $21,000 in Dunfield's venture. And, like other searchers before him, he soaked up information from Reginald V. Harris' book and from sources at the Nova Scotia Archives. He also gained a lot of first-hand information by talking with Hedden, Hamilton, and Chappell.

There seems to be no end to the succession of risk-takers who are willing to stake their lives and fortunes on Oak Island; when Dunfield dropped out in 1966, Blankenship took over. He envisaged a careful and comprehensive drilling program to be followed by a well thought-out excavation, which he felt was sure to succeed.

At the outset, Blankenship first commuted on a seasonal basis between Florida and Nova Scotia, spending his winters in Miami with his wife and children. Finally, in 1975, he moved them to the Island where he built his present home. But he needed a backer and was fortunate to quickly team up with David Tobias, a packaging and label manufacturer from Montreal who had previously invested in Restall's expedition. Tobias, then in his early 40s, was a well-established businessman who was able to attract wealthy investors. He formed Triton Alliance Limited in April 1969 with himself as president and Blankenship as field operation director. The shareholders included Charles Brown, a prosperous Boston land developer; George Jennison, a past president of the Toronto Stock Exchange; Bill Sobey, chairman of a large supermarket chain; Bill Parkins, a weapons designer for the United States Pentagon; Gordon Coles, a former Nova Scotia Attorney-General; and Mel Chappell, owner of the Money Pit area, holder of the treasure trove license, and member of Triton's board of directors.

But before Triton Alliance was formed, Blankenship and Tobias carried out a substantial search. In 1966 they deepened Dunfield's south shore shaft in a further search for the second flood tunnel. At a depth of about 60 feet they uncovered an "ancient hand-wrought nail and something that resembled a "nut or washer." At 90 feet down they found "a layer of round granite stones about the size of a man's head." The rocks were laying in a pool of stagnant water and Blankenship was positive that they had intercepted a portion of the south shore flood system. They spent several months trying to crib and deepen the shaft until the work was abandoned when soil collapsed into the hole.

In 1967 Blankenship dug up sections of the beach at Smith's Cove and found coconut fiber, which botanists confirmed was authentic, and the remains of the old drainage system. Among his discoveries was a pair of wrought iron scissors found beneath one of the feeder drains. The scissors were examined by a former curator of the Smithsonian's Historical Archaeology division who said they were of a 300-year-old pattern and "could be that old," but also could be of fairly recent construction. Considering where they were found, the former is more likely.

Other items found under the beach at Smith's Cove included a heart-shaped stone determined to have been chiseled, and an old set square which metallurgists dated to a period prior to 1780.

In 1970, after Triton Alliance was formed, a 400-foot long soil cofferdam was constructed around the perimeter of Smith's Cove. It was situated about 50 feet further out to sea than the dams of the early years but, like them, it too was destroyed by Atlantic storms. However, its construction yielded a significant discovery.

A large U-shaped wooden structure was uncovered below low tide. It was made of several large two-foot-thick logs ranging from 30 to 65 feet in length. The logs were notched at four foot intervals and a Roman numeral was carved beside each notch (each numeral being different). The notches had been bored and several contained two-inch-thick wooden dowels. The notches and dowels were thought to have secured cross pieces between the logs. Experts concluded that the structure was an ancient wharf or slipway or the remains of workings used in the construction of an original cofferdam to hold back the sea while the flood system to the Money Pit was being constructed.

Over the years since Blankenship and Tobias began, a lot of their efforts have centered around an extensive drilling program. In the year 1967 alone, they drilled approximately 60 holes in the area of the Money

The Halifax Herald Ltd.

Daniel Blankenship working on drill hole casing. An extensive drilling program indicates caverns or tunnels deep in the Island's bedrock.

William S. Crooker

Triton Alliance drilling operation near Money Pit; August 1976.

163

Pit. From these operations they learned that there are caverns or tunnels in the bedrock deep below the Island with ceilings of wood planks or logs. These cavities were discovered about 40 feet down in the bedrock which was found to begin about 160 feet below the ground surface or about 170 feet below the "original surface." (About 12 feet of the overburden soil had been removed by Dunfield in 1965, so the drillers recorded depths less than originally existed. The approximate 160 foot depth is also said to vary ten feet either way in some places.)

In the course of drilling, pieces of china, cement, wood, charcoal, metal, and oak buds were brought up in locations varying from 170 to 222 feet from the original grade. On striking the tunnels or caverns, the drill would first cut down through 30 or 40 feet of bedrock which consisted mostly of anhydrite containing varying amounts of gypsum and then hit two layers of wood each several inches thick, separated by a thin layer of blue clay. The drill would then drop down through a void between six to eight feet deep before again striking bedrock.

Tobias told me that wood brought up from the deep levels was carbon dated at 1575 plus or minus 85 years. (Carbon dating is a method of establishing the approximate age of carbonaceous remains such as wood by measuring the amount of radioactive carbon-14 remaining.) He also said that carbon dating had determined that the coconut fiber from the beach at Smith's Cove was older than the wood. Tobias shied away from discussing the age difference, so I questioned Dan Blankenship. Dan said that he didn't profess to be an expert on the subject but he felt that carbon dating wasn't particularly well suited for determining the age of such a "late" substance. He didn't go into details as to why it wasn't well suited but said that he felt that carbon dating was more applicable to a substance dating back a thousand years or more.

In search of some logical explanation for the age discrepancy, I talked with Harold Krueger of Krueger Enterprises, Inc., Geochron Laboratories Division of Cambridge, Massachusetts, who had carbon dated wood samples for Triton Alliance. Krueger remembered conducting carbon-14 analysis work for Triton in the late 1960s. He informed me that the estimate of the age of an oak when killed can be out by 200 years or more, depending on what part of the stem the sample is taken from. For example, let's suppose that a 250-year oak was cut down in 1750 and used to shore up the roof of a cavern under Oak Island. A drill brings up a chip from the center of the oak in the year 2000 and the approximate age of the sample is correctly analyzed as 500 years. It is not known that the tree had 250 rings of growth when it died and the sample is not from its surface. (The lab always recommends that samples be taken from the surface of the trunk of a tree for the sake of accuracy.) Not taking the possible variance into consideration, the underground work is errone- ously dated 1500 based on the year 2000. With regard to the carbon dated age of 1575 plus or minus 85 years, Krueger said that there is a 67 percent probability that the true age falls within the range of 1490 to 1660. For a higher confidence level of 95 percent, it is necessary to double the range to plus or minus 170 years (1405–1745) and approxi- mately triple the 85 plus or minus range for a 99 percent level of confidence. Krueger's information doesn't provide an answer to why the coconut fiber predates the wood but it does throw a little light on the carbon dating process.

On questioning Tobias about the unusual discovery of wood and cavities down in the bedrock, he said, "The oak samples were quite understandably found at the 200-foot level. No one would have built a vault above the bedrock where it could easily be reached."

Fred Nolan told me that Triton encountered a cavern near the Money Pit in 1969 while he was doing survey work for the drilling operation. "They drilled to a depth of 210 feet at the Money Pit and struck a plug of blue clay down in the bedrock. The bedrock was 165 feet down. Blankenship and Tobias figured that the cavern was man-made but it isn't, as far as I'm concerned."

The interesting part of Nolan's statement is the "plug of blue clay." Nolan thinks that the plug of clay may have originated from the 1861 collapse of the Money Pit. "It apparently fell into the cavern from above," he said. "This plug of blue clay was unlike any found on the Island and was probably the plug that stopped the water from the artificial drain from Smith's Cove." Nolan theorized that the plug of clay was a seal that had been broken when the Onslow company of 1803 removed the inscribed stone. He figured that when they removed the stone and dug down, they probably broke the seal, which let in the water.

In the course of carrying out drilling programs, one drill hole became a shaft that received considerable public attention because of the sensationalism it stirred up. The shaft, designated Borehole 10-X and situated 180 feet northeast of the Money Pit, began as just another six-inch diameter drill hole but the drillers encountered cavities that prompted Triton to concentrate its efforts on this spot.

In the initial probe, they discovered five-foot-deep cavities at 140 and 160-foot depths, bedrock at 180 feet, and another cavity at 230 feet. They brought up small quantities of metal from the 165-foot level which encouraged Triton to enlarge the hole to 27 inches in diameter down to the lowest cavity at 230 feet. In drilling the wider hole, pieces of wood, metal, chain, and broken wire came up. The hole also filled to sea level with salt water and pieces of bird bones, seashells, and glass came to the surface indicating a connection with the flood system to the Money Pit.

Encouraged by their findings, Triton decided to explore the deepest cavity with an underwater remote-controlled television camera. They lowered the camera to a depth of 230 feet while Blankenship watched a closed-circuit monitor in a nearby shack. At first there was nothing but "snow" to be seen on the screen but suddenly there appeared what seemed to be the faint outlines of three chests, one with a handle on the end and a curved top, a pick-axe, and three logs lying on the floor of the chamber. The next view was gruesome. It showed what appeared to be a human hand—half-clenched and severed at the wrist. It hung suspended for a few minutes in front of the camera lens before it disappeared when it was accidentally struck by the camera and driven out of sight. And then the camera picked up what appeared to be a human body slumped in a sitting position against the side of one of the walls of the cavern.

Photographs that were taken with a flash camera of the TV screen are said to lack the necessary clarity to be conclusive and they were later minimized because of the unknown scale factor. As Tobias reportedly said, "They could have been anything."

Triton then hired a diving company. Several dives were made to the bottom cavern which was reported to be about seven feet deep. Its horizontal expanse couldn't be determined due to poor visibility caused by the murkiness of the water.

Bore Hole 10-X was later increased to a diameter of about eight feet and it was extended downward with the hope of finding a tunnel to the Money Pit, without positive results. The cavities at 140 feet and 160 feet were found to be natural and probably only pockets created by sand blown away by the original churn drilling. The bottom void at 230 feet

Steel cylinders used in the construction of casing for Borehole 10-X.

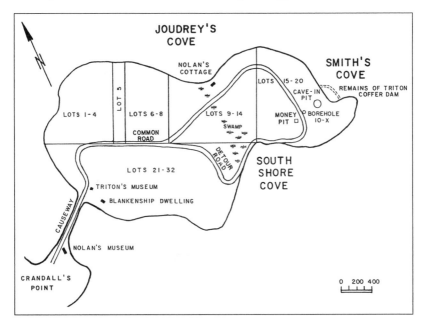

Diagram of Oak Island; 1993.

was indicated by sonar surveying equipment to have no tunnel leading to it and therefore it was assumed to be natural.

Work on Bore Hole 10-X eventually gave way to a plan of attack on the Money Pit and Triton sent out its prospectus to Canadian and United States underwriters early in the winter of 1988. Tobias had expected to have the financing in place and the dig underway by early in the summer of that year but, as he told me on January 9, 1992, "Black Monday" (the October 19, 1987, stock market crash) had a devastating effect on their financing plans.

In 1991 Triton made a major approach to the government for financial support. It applied to the Atlantic Canada Opportunities Agency in the summer of that year for a $12 million loan guarantee. The application promised the creation of 50 jobs and suggested a substantial spinoff in tourism opportunities. However, the application was rejected because it fell outside the Atlantic Canada Opportunities Agency guidelines and therefore didn't qualify for support.

Triton had also hoped to find allies in the Department of Tourism but the Minister of Tourism, Greg Kerr, is quoted to have said, "The Triton Alliance project is a treasure hunt and the Department of Tourism and Culture does not fund that kind of thing. The project requires substantial financial investment which has not been obtained."

Politicians generally feel that the risk is too great. Colchester MLA, Ed Lorraine may have summed up the feelings of many when he said, "With the financial mess this province and country is already in, we shouldn't give them a nickel. If they're so certain there's treasure down there, let them convince the banks."

TWENTY-ONE

The Christian Cross

"**I** have undisputed proof that the Money Pit is a decoy. The proof is over on my property and it's conclusive. It makes the Money Pit a small project in comparison to what I've found." It was Fred Nolan speaking from across the coffee table on June 17, 1992, as I sat gazing at the photograph of a large rock that resembled the shape of a human skull.

Nolan had called me eight days earlier on June 9th, around 10:30 a.m., asking to meet later that morning. On the phone he told me he wanted to discuss something that might be of considerable interest to me; he had made a breakthrough and was considering going forward with an excavation. He knew I was in the throes of writing a new book on Oak Island and suggested that arrangements might be made whereby I would get exclusive rights on all information pertaining to the new dig. Well, of course I was interested! Since our homes and work places are only about ten miles apart, his in Bedford and mine on the outskirts of Halifax, we met a half-hour later for coffee in a restaurant near the edge

The Head Stone, a startling clue in the unresolved mystery.

of the city. We sat and sipped coffee for two hours while Nolan introduced his discovery.

"I've been surveying and searching for over 30 years," he said, "and I'm in the process of piecing together some substantial discoveries into a cohesive theory."

Nolan explained that he had found many survey markers that looked natural to the layman, although they proved to be man-made. For years, he ran survey lines through points he had found and one line would frequently intersect another, resulting in still another discovery. "I would find two markers and project a line through them and find a third but at that time it didn't make any sense," he said. However, as time went by the pieces of the puzzle began to fall into place. But when he finally arrived at the juncture where his discoveries suggested a solution to the mystery, he couldn't share it. "I needed something of a substantial nature to show," Nolan said. "I needed something that people would be able to understand and relate to, and now I have it."

Obviously, if Nolan was going to undertake a major excavation he probably required backers. It would be difficult to attract investors on the basis of a series of survey markers, many of which appeared to be nothing more than natural splinters of rock. I understood his problem. But I left our little meeting with no information other than that he had found "something great and man-made," as he had described it. He wasn't prepared to disclose his discovery. "I still haven't quite made up my mind if I want to share this with the public," he said, as we shook hands in the restaurant lobby.

But Nolan had apparently "made up his mind" on that evening of June 17th. He told me to take the photograph of the rock which he had dubbed "the Head Stone" and show it to anyone. "See what they say," he suggested. Then he let me in on his find.

Nolan explained that the rock survey markers were intended to appear natural so that no one would "get tipped off" and go searching for the treasure. They were only supposed to be meaningful to the people who put them there but were also meaningful to him because when he ran lines through unquestionably artificial things such as anchor bolts in rocks, he intercepted these markers. Some of these markers were not hand-worked in any way, but were obviously hand-placed due to the abnormal positions in which they were found. They were not laying in a natural state. Rather, they were positioned "straight up" with "a pointed end protruding through the surface of the ground."

Nolan recounted that he would find two or three survey markers in one location and two or three in another but they made no sense until he tied them together by running lines between them in all directions. "I would go to sleep at night wondering what I might learn by joining one point to another. Then I would go out to the Island the next day and survey for the answer," Nolan reminisced. He said that when he took measurements between markers, he was looking for some measurement or measurements that fit a "pattern." He was looking for a meaningful measurement that could be applied and eventually he found it. "I felt that all those markers had to mean something," Nolan said. "The trick was to discover or figure out the pattern they represented."

Now, after years of investigation, Nolan claims to have discovered a pattern for all of the markers he surveyed. He says they form a mathematical equation. It is an equation that involves trigonometry but very strangely it also involves symbolism. And, that is where the Head Stone fits in!

Nolan said that the Head Stone was laying on its side when he discovered it. The side or face of the stone was slightly slanted with the top portion or head exposed. He dug it up with a backhoe and photographed it. At that point in time it meant nothing more to him than just another rock to be examined. But it was a rock that shouldn't have been there. It was composed of sandstone and bore glacial striation lines which indicated that it had once been part of a bedrock formation. Of course this could have been a fluke of nature but as Nolan later discovered, it wasn't.

Nolan asked if I noticed anything else peculiar about the Head Stone other than its human skull shape and the glacial striations. There were scratches on the rock which had obviously been clawed by the teeth of the backhoe bucket and there was what appeared to be a well-weathered slot or groove on the face. Nolan said the groove was hand-carved in the shape of the very same dagger that he had acquired from the heirs of Sophia Sellers, daughter of Anthony Graves. (The Graves who had once occupied Nolan's property.) He said it was a "perfect fit," and concluded that the Head Stone symbolically represented "the brain" and the dagger pointed to the "heart"—the brain and heart of the equation.

On that bizarre twist to his story, Nolan turned to the physical nature of the survey markers or monuments. He explained that there was a vast scale differential. Some were average size survey monuments such as the "Spanish Galleon" shaped stone, while others were very large. "You could be leaning against one and never recognize it as a survey monument," Nolan said. "The Head Stone is, in fact, a survey monument, regardless of its size."

With that, Nolan concluded all that he was prepared to discuss that evening, He changed the subject and proposed that I transport my survey equipment over to the Island to conduct a survey of a few of the markers. He explained that he wanted an engineer to check some of his measurements and verify his findings, now that he was prepared to go public with an astounding discovery. He said he would have the press on hand while my survey was being conducted. They could take pictures and he would be available to answer any of their questions.

On winding up our meeting, I asked Nolan what the Head Stone and this mysterious equation with a symbolic meaning "was really all about." Nolan said that the answer had to be supported by the evidence. Regarding the mystery of his findings, Nolan said on closing, "If I told someone what the answer to the puzzle is, they would think I was crazy."

A month following our June 17th meeting, I sat on a sofa in the reception room of Nolan's museum on Crandall's Point, holding a plot plan which showed the configuration of the most ancient and symbolic image known to man—a cross! It resembled a giant Latin cross or crucifix. Each arm of the cross, which Nolan has dubbed the "Christian Cross," was shown as 360 feet in length and the total length of the stem from top to bottom was 867 feet. The ends of the arms and the top and bottom of the stem each terminated at a circle marked by the word "cone" and the base stem was also divided by a circle marked "cone" at a distance of 293 feet from the bottom. The center of the cross (where the arms meet the stem) was marked "headstone."

At the left-hand bottom corner of the plot was a diagram of a cone entitled "cone boulder size," indicating that the cones were rocks. It was shown as being eight feet wide at the base and nine feet high.

The cross shown on the plot plan was almost perfectly proportioned. Within two feet, the body (the portion of the stem from the Head Stone to the bottom) was twice the length of either arm. Within three feet, the top (the portion of the stem from the Head Stone to the top) was five times the length of the body and twice the distance of the bottom cone of the body to the cone situated partway up the body. These almost numerically even ratios of body to arms and top to body suggested to me that what Nolan had found was not an accident of nature.

We were waiting for the press as I studied Nolan's plot plan and squeezed out the impressive ratios on a pocket calculator. The meeting had been arranged for 1:00 p.m. but Nolan got held up in traffic and was a half-hour late. Meanwhile, the press arrived, gave Nolan 15 minutes grace, and left. We figured that perhaps the newspeople might have gone for a quick lunch and would be back, so we waited. And while we waited Nolan talked about the Cross and the artifacts he had discovered.

Nolan said that he had discovered the Head Stone and the five cone-

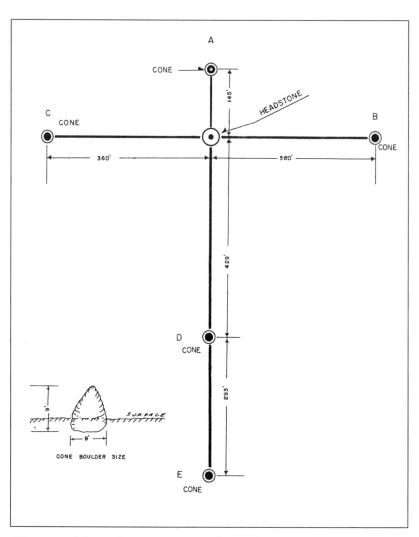

Diagram of the "Christian Cross," obviously a manmade clue to the mystery of Oak Island.

shaped boulders in 1981 but Triton's civil suit against him curtailed his operations on the Island for a decade. He was only now getting to the point of disclosing the discovery to the public. Asked why he had decided to go public with this discovery, Nolan said, "I hate to share all this after 30 years of work but if I die without telling anyone, all my work will be lost. I could be driving down the highway tomorrow and get killed in an accident. No one would ever know about the Cross." Then he showed me a photograph of an artifact that he believes is associated with the Cross. It is a lock with a cross-shaped keyhole. When the key is turned, the face opens and another smaller keyhole appears. He didn't disclose where he found the lock but it may have been among various items recovered in a hole dug near the north shore at Joudrey's Cove. He had dug down about six feet and found pieces of dishes and culinary such as knives and forks.

Nolan described another artifact, in which he says Blankenship was quite interested, "a pair of very old handmade scissors, forged by a blacksmith." He found the scissors embedded in earth near one of the 30-foot deep shafts he had dug between 1963 and 1964. The scissors, made of wrought-iron, are not identical to the pair that Blankenship found at Smith's Cove but are "somewhat alike in configuration."

The most interesting artifact that Nolan described in terms of size is a railway trolley with wheels that run on a track. It lay buried beneath the mud in the swamp and he had hauled it out with a timber jack. He can only guess that it may have been rolled out on the ice during the winter and then sunk into the deep mud in the spring. It may have been owned by Anthony Graves or Henry Sellers or one of the Sellers heirs and simply discarded by disposing of it in the swamp. Or is it a piece of the Oak Island puzzle?

Among other artifacts found in the swamp, Nolan showed me an old

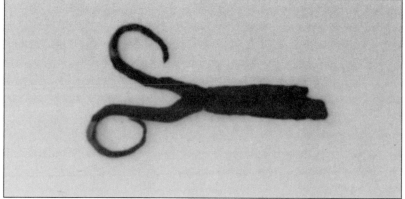

William S. Crooker

Wrought-iron scissors found on Nolan's property are similar to those found near the Money Pit.

piece of wood off the side of a sailing ship containing grooves through which ropes had once been attached. He said that extensive probing when the swamp was drained in 1969 showed no evidence of a ship having been buried beneath the mud. Another item of interest Nolan recovered from the swamp is an old branding iron. About 12 inches long, it has an iron handle but the branding protrusion marks are badly worn, making interpretation difficult if not impossible.

The press had not returned by 1:45 p.m. so we launched Nolan's 12-foot aluminum boat and loaded it up with the necessary survey equipment to include transit, tripods, range poles, and electronic distance measuring equipment.

On the way over to the Island, Nolan complained that Oak Island has seriously harmed his survey business. "People have lost respect for me because I'm a treasure hunter," he said, "and they question my judgment. As an expert witness in court I have had lawyers try to discredit me by asking if I searched for treasure as if that was a mark against me." Perhaps Nolan had hoped that press coverage of a substantial discovery would erase his supposed credibility problem.

It was low tide when the bow of the boat scraped the rocky bottom of Joudrey's Cove. I was seated in the middle and so I hopped out to lighten the load, pulling the boat partly up onto the beach. Nolan tilted up the outboard motor and tied the bow rope to a boulder near high water. "The land is alive," he joked, "You have to be sure you tie up high enough."

"Well, Bill, there is the first cone," Nolan said, pointing to a large conical-shaped granite boulder about the size of a compact automobile and situated between high and low tides about 40 feet below the high water mark of the shore. Nolan noted that this boulder is the cone lettered "C" on the left end of the arm of the Cross shown on his plot plan.

Nolan explained that the body or stem of the cross straddles the swamp with the top cone and Head Stone on the east side and the two bottom cones on the west, all on dry land; the stem of the cross runs in a southwest to northeast direction from the bottom to the top; the arms are at right angles to the stem and run northwest to southeast from the cone on Joudrey's Cove.

Nolan then said that he thinks the Cross was laid out with the English system of measurements and that the distance of 360 feet from the ends

William S. Crooker

Cone-shaped boulder on the beach of Jodrey's Cove (Cone "C" on plot plan), one of a series that forms the Cross.

of the arms to the Head Stone corresponds to the number of degrees in a circle. (He apparently feels strongly about his contention that the cross was laid out in feet because he was annoyed by a future press release in which the reporter converted the measurements to meters.) The ratios were of the utmost interest to me so it really didn't matter what unit of measurement was used as these ratios remain unaffected. I agreed to conduct the survey using the Imperial rather than the Metric system.

After giving me a general idea of the layout and on the system of measurements to be used, Nolan took me for a tour of the Cross. We walked inland past the east end of his cottage and crossed the old road leading to the Money Pit. A short distance south of the old road, Nolan stopped and pointed to a slab of sandstone almost flush with the ground. "There's the Head Stone," he said. It looked like the bottom of a large dish, partly covered with topsoil and grass. The stone had been dug up, examined, photographed, and then laid back on its side with the face almost flush with the ground, after a little back-filling to preserve the stone. "It's not in the exact position where we found it," Nolan said. "We didn't know what it meant at the time so we laid it aside a few feet. We were planning to dig a shaft here but we referenced its original position." Nolan pointed to an iron bar protruding a few inches out of the ground. "That is in the exact location of the center of the cheek below the point of the dagger," he said.

The granite boulder at the end of the south arm of the Cross, lettered "B" on the plot plan, was about the same size and shape as the one at the shore. Even though it had been tipped over, the indenture in the ground at its original position was clear. Nolan said they discovered the remains of a wrought iron stove under the rock when they rolled it over and exposed its bottom. He also said they found small beach stones under the rock. John C. O'Keefe, a retired gentleman of East Uniacke, Nova Scotia, who had worked with Nolan on the Island, recalls: "There's a big rock up there in the field, a great big boulder. We took the bulldozer and the backhoe and rolled it over and out of the way and there underneath were pieces of an old wrought iron pot bellied stove, right there on top and as we dug down we found other pieces. The pieces were beveled and as we dug them up you could see it was a pot bellied stove…. How it ever got down there is beyond me…. Fred was really surprised and we kept digging and digging and found other pieces of stuff there, too, like knives and forks. I don't know how a big rock ever got on top of all that. Why would someone go to all the trouble of digging a hole, burying all that stuff and then rolling a big rock like that over it? It just doesn't make any sense." (O'Keefe didn't know about the discovery of the Cross configuration at the time of the interview so he had no notion as to why the boulder might have found a place above the buried items.)

I questioned O'Keefe about the presence of beach stones under the rock and he said, "There were beach stones all over the place, actually. There were beach stones in several holes we dug and there could have been some under the big rock but I can't remember for sure."

Continuing the tour of the Cross, Nolan showed me the cone-shaped stones on the stem. They were all similar in shape and size to the one at the beach. The two lower cones of the stem were undisturbed but the top one was misplaced by about 20 feet. It had held no significance to Nolan when it was discovered and disturbed but fortunately the depression in the ground where it had once rested was clearly visible, making it possible to estimate the original position of the top of the cone. From the depression to the stone was a trail that had been made by tractor treads and the dragging of a large heavy object. Nolan said that the stone had been in the way of a line he was running, and had told the machine operator to drag it out of the way.

Asked how many other boulders of similar size and shape might be found on the Island, Nolan said there were no others. He said that on surveying the entire Island in 1961–1962, he had not seen any granite boulders of the size and configuration that mark off the Cross. During my tour of the Cross, I looked around for boulders of a similar shape. I saw only one rock of the size of the cones but it was far from being conical. There were boulders on the shore of Joudrey's Cove but a cursory search turned up nothing resembling the cones of the Cross.

Proceeding with my assignment, I estimated the original positions of the tops of the two cone-shaped boulders that had been disturbed, and carried out the survey. The arms of the Cross were indeed at right angles to the stem and all the measurements complied with Nolan's plot plan!

It now appears obvious that someone in the past spent a large amount of time and labor laying out the configuration of a large Latin cross on Oak Island. The cone-shaped stones were apparently hand selected, probably from boulders on the shores, and weigh about ten tons each. To transport these stones into position would have required a large work force using skids and even with the aid of horses or oxen, would have been quite labor intensive. The work may have been conducted during the winter but even with the advantage of sliding the boulders on skids over frozen ground, the work would have been difficult. And the boulders would have had to been surveyed into place by engineers.

There must have been a scheme behind all the work of building the Cross and Nolan believes it bears a relationship to a large deposit beneath his swamp which he says is "the real treasure." Who's to say he is wrong? The Cross doesn't seem to mark the location of the Money Pit. Lines drawn through the cones in every conceivable direction fail to intercept anywhere close to the Pit.

Considering Nolan's findings, if the long-sought treasure lies under his swamp, why was the Money Pit dug? Nolan believes it's a decoy. Although it seems incredible that anyone would build a system as complex as the Money Pit and its flood trap just to throw treasure

Cone-shaped boulder on stem of Cross. (Cone "D" on plot plan.)

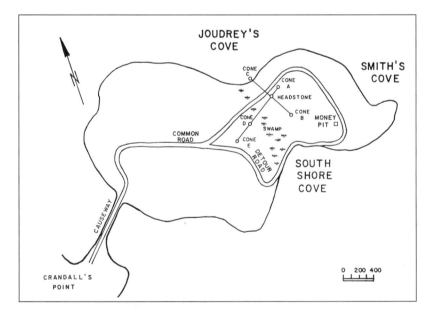

Diagram of Oak Island showing size and location of Cross.

hunters off track, he may have a point. According to a long-standing theory, inclined tunnels were excavated from deep down in the Money Pit to points 20 or 30 feet below ground surface and some distance away from the Pit, perhaps hundreds of feet. Watertight vaults keyed to surface markers were constructed at the ends of the tunnels and the treasure was distributed among them. The tunnels and Money Pit shaft were then back-filled and the tidal flood trap was activated. If this theory is true, the Money Pit did serve as a decoy although not built specifically for that purpose. Nolan says, "I may be wrong but there's one thing that's indisputable. The Money Pit has kept searchers busy in the same location for two centuries."

David Tobias and Dan Blankenship of Triton Alliance aren't saying they share Nolan's belief that a treasure lies beneath his property. However, in September 1992, after the press released a story about the Cross in July, Nolan says Triton drafted a proposal permitting him to drive out to his land in return for sharing information about his discoveries, providing copies of his maps with a profile of the swamp, and 30 percent cut of any treasure recovered.

On October 3, 1992, I made my last visit to the Island before completing this book. I went there to photograph the cone-shaped stones and other markers Nolan had found.

Nolan was there that day to dig but he spent his time working on the drain spouts on the eaves of his cottage until I finished my work. As I was leaving, he carried a battery over to his backhoe and began to connect it up. As he turned a wrench on one of the bolts connecting a wire to a battery terminal, I asked my final question. "Is there anything particularly significant about the way in which the markers are laid out that we may not have discussed?" Nolan thought for a moment and then replied, "Well, there is, at least in my opinion. The accuracy applied to the measurements and the manner in which they were planted or installed smacks very much of a military operation!"

TWENTY-TWO

The
Templar
Speculations

On Saturday July 18, 1992, four days after my survey of the Cross, *The Halifax Herald* reported a new discovery on Oak Island, based on an interview with Fred Nolan. The article stirred up considerable public interest and Nolan was flooded with telephone calls. Since I had conducted the survey and was in the throes of writing a new book about Oak Island, Nolan referred the callers to me.

Aside from trying to uncover additional information about the Cross, the investigators put forth their theories about the Cross' origins. They all seemed to think that the Cross, in some mystical way, related to the medieval Order of the Knights Templar or the modern-day Masons.

These same Oak Island observers contacted me a few more times and in the course of several lengthy conversations I began to learn why they were thinking this way. They were drawing heavily from two recent books, *The Holy Blood and the Holy Grail* by Michael Baigent, Richard

Leigh, and Henry Lincoln, and *Holy Grail Across the Atlantic* by
Michael Bradley.

According to these books, the story unfolds.... The Knights Templar
was founded in 1118 A.D. under the name of the Order of the Poor
Knights of Christ and the Temple of Solomon, 19 years after the capture
of the Holy City during the First Christian Crusade. It was a shadowy
order of warrior-monks who played a very crucial role in the Christian
Crusades, fighting and dying by the thousands. These monks, dressed
in white capes with splayed red crosses, were the storm troopers in the
siege of the Holy Land. They fought to reclaim the sepulcher of Jesus
Christ and the Holy Land from the Muslim infidels.

The Templars had made pledges to obedience, poverty, and chastity
and their sole allegiance was to the Pope. They were thus totally
independent of the rule of any king, prince, or prelate. Admission to the
Order required that the new recruit sign over all possessions. The
Templar's holdings proliferated as the sons of noble families throughout Europe flocked to the Order. As well, wealthy Crusade supporters
donated vast amounts of money, goods, and land. While the Order
welcomed all the donations and gifts with open arms, it disposed of
nothing. The Order's constitution disallowed any form of divestiture
even for noble causes such as to ransom a leader.

It was the Templars who established the institution of modern
banking, and this industrious order became the bankers for every
throne in Europe by lending large sums to destitute monarchs. They
came to own their own seaports, shipyards, and fleet.

As well as amassing great wealth, the Templars became a powerful
organization with strong international influences, acting often as me-
diators between nobles and monarchs throughout the Western world
and the Holy Land. But their wealth, influence, and independence were
to be short-lived.

By 1306 the Crusades were over and the Holy Land had fallen almost
entirely under Muslim control. The Templars had lost their *raison
d'etre* and King Philip IV of France was determined to rid his country
of the Order. They had a military force much stronger than his; they
were arrogant and unruly; they were firmly established throughout his
country; and, perhaps above all, he owed them a lot of money. With the
Pope's support, King Philip compiled a list of charges which were in
part derived from information provided by the king's spies who had

A Templar: keepers of the Holy Grail?

infiltrated the Order. Armed with sufficient accusations to deliver his blow, the king issued secret orders to his agents throughout the country stipulating a simultaneous arrest of all the Templars in France at dawn on Friday, October 13, 1307. Furthermore, all of their estates and goods were to be confiscated for the Crown. Even though a number of knights escaped the dragnet, the arrest was largely successful. But Philip failed in his main objective: to acquire the Templar's immense wealth. The Templar's treasure had mysteriously disappeared.

According to rumor, the Order had received advance warning of the planned arrest and they arranged to have the treasure smuggled by night from Parisian estates and transported by wagons to the coast and finally to the Templar's naval base at LaRochelle. There, the fortune was loaded onto 18 galleys and shipped off to sea—never to be heard from again.

The curious folks who had phoned me about the Cross speculated that the treasure might have ended up buried on Oak Island. But that is only one of many versions of the story connecting the Knights Templar to the treasure hunt.

Although the Pope officially dissolved the Knights Templar in 1312 under pressure by the King, the Order wasn't completely wiped out. A number of knights remained at large—either by acquittal or through escape—and the Order went underground. Philip's attempts to persuade his fellow European monarchs to help eliminate the Order were unsuccessful. While some Templars were arrested in England, most received only light sentences such as a few years of penance in an abbey or monastery.

Many knights found refuge in Scotland which was at war with England at the time. According to legend, the Order maintained itself as a coherent body in Scotland for another 400 years. In the Lorraine section of Germany, the Order was supported by the duke of the principality, while in Portugal, the Order simply modified its name to "Kings of Christ" and continued on well into the 1500s.

Although the connection between Oak Island and the Templars may seem tenuous, the folks who phoned me that day to discuss the Cross had done their homework. They point out that Henry Sinclair of Scotland (who they believe was a Templar) visited Nova Scotia in 1398, a date established by the American historian and author, Frederick Pohl. They figure that Sinclair arrived to either conceal or recover the treasure of the Templars. After several months of exploration, he built

*Sketch of the Sinclair
Arms. Henry Sinclair,
thought to have been a
Templar, may have built
a castle at New Ross,
N.S., in 1398.*

a refuge castle at New Ross, about 17 miles from Oak Island, in the
watershed area of the Gold River. And he proceeded to plant the oaks
on Oak Island to serve as a beacon for future refugees in search of his
castle. Since it would be the only island bearing oak trees, all the refugee
had to do was to find it and then follow Gold River which emptied into
the bay only two miles to the north. As for the Money Pit, it was to serve
as a temporary repository for the treasure that was to be transported to
the island refuge. Alternatively, the Money Pit was deemed to be a vault

to hold the gold that was panned from Gold River, destined for European markets.

Others speculate that the Oak Island oaks were planted hundreds of years before Sinclair's visit, and that the castle had been built at that same time. According to this version of the tale, Sinclair knew of the whereabouts of the oak-treed island and the river that ran down from a refuge castle. When he arrived, he found the castle in ruins but proceeded to build a new one on its foundation.

The idea that there was a castle at New Ross is not without some support. In 1979 I received a letter from a lady in New Ross who said that she and her husband had bought a house in that village in 1972 that "stands on a castle mound [the ruins of a castle]." She was unable to find anyone to authenticate her discovery. The lady and her husband have since moved away and this fragment of history has yet to be pursued.

After offering their speculations on the Knights Templar and Henry Sinclair and his castle, the investigators brought up the subject of the modern-day Masons. They astutely noted that several high-ranking Masons of the 20th century have been associated with Oak Island, which brought to mind names like Frederick Blair, Gilbert Hedden, George W. Grimm Jr. (Hedden's New Jersey lawyer), Mel Chappell, and Reginald V. Harris—all members of the Masonic Lodge. Did they have a secret connection with the medieval Knights Templar and its vast treasure? The authors of *The Holy Blood and the Holy Grail* assert that some Masonic lodges have added the level of "Templar" to rituals and appellations said to have been passed down from the original Order of the Knights Templar. They also note that at least three contemporary organizations call themselves Templars. In a letter to George W. Grimm, Jr. dated November 5, 1963, Reginald V. Harris makes mention of a Templar Order. Harris writes: "I got away for a few days to the Knights Templar Assembly at Montreal, in August...."

The Investigators feel that the Cross of Oak Island may have a religious meaning connected with secrets held by the Masons, and that if there is a treasure on Oak Island, it is likely to contain religious material of untold significance for future generations.

Indeed, the Templars are believed to have been the custodians of some great treasure as well as holders of a momentous secret from the Christian tradition. Indeed, we know that Templar-inspired secret societies endure to the present day.

Iconography of the Masons, descendents of the Templars.

The authors of *The Holy Blood and the Holy Grail* attempt to unravel the great secret that has been protected by the Templars. Rather than being the cup or platter used by Jesus Christ at the Last Supper and by Joseph of Arimathea to collect drops of Jesus' blood at the crucifixion, they believe that the Holy Grail is a lineage, pedigree, or bloodline of people. Jesus Christ was part of that bloodline, either from birth or through marriage. He fathered children thus making the bloodline "holy." His wife Mary Magdalene and offspring fled the Holy Land, found a refuge in southern France, and preserved their lineage in a Jewish community. Rather than being a physical object, the Holy Grail is a symbol of Jesus' bloodline and his wife's womb from which the bloodline came forth.

By 1100 Jesus' descendents had risen to a state of great prominence in Europe and also in Palestine. They knew their pedigree and ancestry but it became necessary for them to prove their bloodline to Jesus. And that proof lay buried beneath the Temple of Solomon. The Knights Templar's original mission was to find it.

A mid-12th-century pilgrim to the Holy Land, Johann von Wuzburg, reportedly saw stables beneath the Temple large enough to accommodate 2,000 horses. As it turned out, the Knights Templar quartered their horses in these stables. It is theorized that these stables were built following a huge excavation by the Templars, in which they found what they were looking for and brought it back to Europe for concealment. About what was concealed, the authors of *The Holy Blood and the Holy Grail* write, "It may have been Jesus' mummified body. It may have been the equivalent, so to speak, of Jesus' marriage licence, and/or the birth certificates of his children. It may have been something of comparable explosive import. Any or all of these items might have been referred to as the Holy Grail." What happened to the Templar's find remains a mystery.

Those investigators who questioned me on the Oak Island Cross believe that the answer to the Holy Grail mystery is buried deep in the Money Pit or elsewhere on the Island.

The fact that a few Oak Island treasure hunters and a couple of their lawyers were Masons is hardly evidence to support such a grandiose scheme. Nor is Henry Sinclair's visit to Nova Scotia and reconstruction of his possible castle at New Ross any firmer evidence of clandestine activity initiated by the Knights Templar.

But what about the Cross? Those who have contacted me about the discovery are adamant that the Cross *must* be connected with a religious organization. They ask, who else but a Templar or a Masonic order would construct a Christian cross? But they may be missing something.

Perhaps the group of cone-shaped rocks and the Head Stone were not laid out to represent a cross. Nolan dubbed the rock configuration the "Christian Cross," and I simply call it the "Cross," but these designations may have led us down the wrong path. If the stones at the ends of the Cross' arms are connected by straight lines to stone "A" at the apex and to one of the stones on the bottom stem, say stone "E," we have four right angled triangles with ratios that may have been significant to those who placed them (see sketch). Within two and one-half

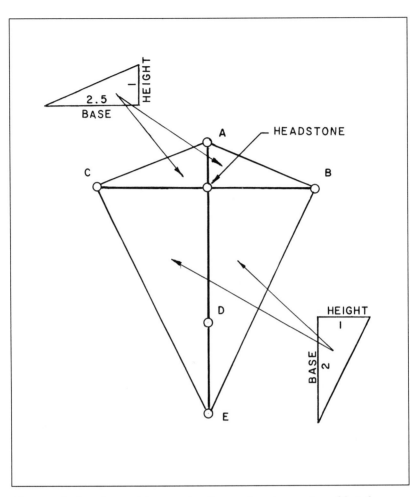

Group of triangles making up the Cross, showing ratios of height to base.

feet, the two identical triangles on the top arms of the Cross have bases that are two and one-half times their height and within two feet, the two identical triangles below the arms have bases that are twice the height. The point common to all four triangles is marked by a stone dissimilar to the others. Instead of being a cone-shaped granite boulder, it is a human head-shaped sandstone. This dissimilarity would have been significant to anyone with a map of the configuration who was about to apply the triangles to locating the deposit. On finding the Head Stone, they would know exactly where they were positioned in relation to the group of triangles.

I have wondered from the outset, when I first saw Nolan's plot plan of his "Christian Cross," why there are two stones on the bottom stem. It then occurred to me that I might be looking at a group of triangles and that either the "D" or "E" cone may only have a geometric or arithmetic significance.

If I was asked to risk money on whether the configuration of stones represent a cross or a group of triangles, I would bet on the latter. However, that bet only makes sense if the configuration doesn't serve a dual purpose.

As well as being a group of triangles, the configuration of stones may utilize the ancient symbol as an instruction in a secret communication. The message may be: Look for a large acorn-shaped granite boulder on the beach at the northern center of the island. That boulder forms the northwestern end of the arm of a large Latin cross marked by similarly shaped stones. Having found it, strike a course in a southeasterly direction for 360 feet and search for a human skull-shaped sandstone which marks the intersection of the arms and the stem of the cross. The searcher is then able to easily find the balance of the cone-shaped boulders, continuing from that stage to apply the geometry of the triangles which correlates with much smaller markers that pinpoint the exact location of one or more deposits.

Some people will not be pleased to hear this theory of what the Cross represents. It is natural to choose a line of speculation in accordance with what we want to believe. The investigators who contacted me want very much to discover an astounding religious revelation on Oak Island. Rather than recognizing a system of markers that takes advantage of the cross motif, they would prefer to see the Cross as a Templar stamp, seal, or brand—an indication that a treasure had been deposited by an order famous for its white mantle emblazoned with a bright red cross.

Collectively, the disappearance of the Templar treasure in 1307, Masons digging on Oak Island, Henry Sinclair's visit to Nova Scotia, and the presence of stones laid in a crucifix pattern provide what the investigators say is circumstantial evidence that Oak Island hides a religious treasure of enormous value.

Like these ferrid souls who carefully constructed their Holy Grail version of the Oak Island whodunit, I too would like to believe that a profound and life-enlightening treasure will ultimately be uncovered. But I am too much of a pragmatist to build a theory on such a weak foundation of circumstantial evidence. And so I continue along a less grandiose path...

TWENTY-THREE

Who?

T he most commonly asked question about Oak Island is "who" buried the treasure. Due to the stupendous nature of the original project, it is almost universally accepted that something of enormous value was deposited and the question of who carried out the original works represents a large part of the mystery. Historians have found no documentation that identifies the mastermind of the project so any plausible answer to the whodunit question has to be deduced from facts, presumptions, logic, and where all else fails, conjecture.

One pragmatic approach to formulating a theory is to establish a "time frame," and then scan the historical scene for the originator.

As a result of Triton Alliance's carbon dating of wood from depths of around 200 feet, some investigators of the mystery suggest a Latin American connection involving the Spanish conquest of the New World, since it falls within that historic time-frame—1575 plus or minus 85 years.

Peruvian goldsmiths at work in front of a house of fine Inca stonework, 1565. What happened to the Inca treasures?

The period of conquest during the 16th and 17th centuries, following the first voyage by Columbus, was an era in which a vast amount of wealth moved from Mexico, Central America, and South America to Spain. That was when the Spanish relieved the Maya, Aztec, and Inca empires of their gold, silver, pearl, and emerald artifacts. When there was nothing left to plunder, the Spanish went straight to the source, the Indian mines, and billions of dollars worth of gold and silver were smelted on-site into ingots and coins.

The route to Spain from the Caribbean usually followed the Gulf Stream up the eastern coast of North America to a latitude north of Bermuda where westerly winds assisted in the homeward voyage. On this course, the convoys often came within three or four hundred miles of Nova Scotia. Some of the cargos were immense, evidenced by the amount of treasure that has been recovered from sunken galleons. The 600-ton *Atocha* that sank off the coast of Florida in 1622 carried

The Spanish plunder of the Americas.

approximately $400 million worth of gold and silver.

Since Nova Scotia was close to the shipping corridor, some people believe that Oak Island served as a temporary government repository for damaged galleons. Other say that a ship became separated from its convoy in a hurricane and found its way to Oak Island where its cargo was buried. The latter suggests that the ship was unloaded of treasure to reduce its weight for the return voyage after temporary repairs. The deposit was made and booby-trapped and the ship headed out to sea but was lost in a storm, along with any record of the event.

Another theory that doesn't involve the Spanish claims the Indians who were being vanquished made a deposit on Oak Island. The most popular story along this vein is that the original work was carried out by the Incas of Tumbes, Peru, around the year 1530. The City of Tumbes was situated on the Pacific coast at the northern tip of Peru, near the southern boarder of Ecuador. It was renowned for its wealth and splendor during the Spanish conquest.

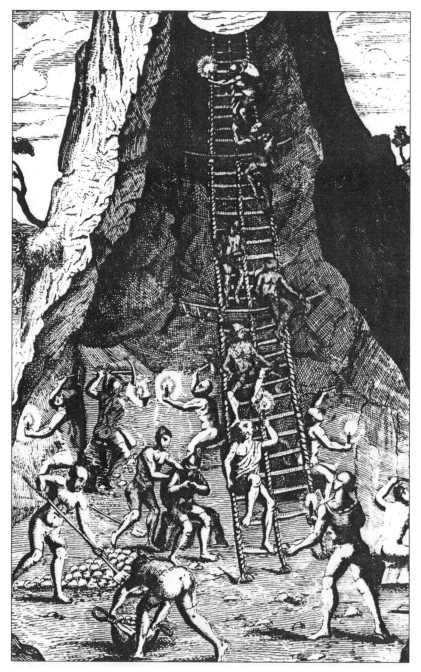

Peruvian mines generated great wealth for Spanish conquerors.

The Spanish conqueror of the Inca Empire, Francisco Pizarro, visited Tumbes in 1527–1528 and coveted everything he saw: a fortified city of astounding wealth filled with utensils and ornaments of gold and silver, huge emeralds, a temple lined with gold, and a palace containing all manner of gold and silver articles. Pizarro went to Spain, gathered up an army, and returned to Tumbes only to find the city in ruins and its enormous treasure missing.

According to legend, the Inca king had all of the city's riches gathered up and transported northward by sea to the Gulf of Panama, a distance of about 900 miles. From there, the Incas backpacked by llama across the Isthmus of Darien to the Caribbean coast. There, the king built or otherwise obtained ships and they set off for a windward island but storms or hurricanes blew them off course and they travelled up the North American coast. Somewhere, far to the north, the fleet found sanctuary and hid the treasure for future recovery. The "Treasure of Tumbes" has never been found.

These theories are colorful but they have certain strikes against them. The problem with Oak Island being used as a repository by the Spanish government or as a temporary hiding place by a stranded ship that underwent repairs is that the area was uninhabited in this era. Since the threat of theft was remote, there would have been no reason to construct such an elaborate "safety deposit box" for a treasure soon to be recovered. If there was a fear of having the cache stolen while away, an armed garrison seems far more logical. As for the Inca hypothesis, it seems fanciful to think that they would travel almost 1,000 miles to the north, cross a land barrier, enter Spanish-infested seas, and travel twice that distance again to bury their riches on an island in a northern area unknown to them.

Other Inca cities were also found to have been stripped of their riches when the conquerors arrived and like Tumbes, the treasures are theorized to be beneath Oak Island. Missing Spanish–American treasures are also rumored to be buried there. But like the other theories, it's only speculation.

Could we be searching in the wrong time slot? Perhaps a clue lies in the early chronicles of the 1795 discovery of the Money Pit.

As might be expected, there are minor variations in the early accounts of the discovery but they do share a common denominator—a clearing in the forest.

One of the earliest accounts of the discovery was written by a member of the Oak Island Association and published in the January 2, 1864 edition of a Halifax newspaper, *The Colonist*. This article states, "He [Daniel McGinnis] found that the first growth of wood had been cut down, and that another was springing up to supply its place. And some old stumps of oak trees that had been chopped down were visible."

Another account in a sworn statement by Adams A. Tupper, who worked on the Island in 1850–1851 and again in 1863, which gives facts related by one of the discovers, Anthony Vaughan, that "It [the clearing in the oak forest] had every appearance of having been cleared many years before."

The records of the discovery are probably reliable. The earliest published versions of the Oak Island story originate from accounts by the three young men who discovered the Money Pit. Two of the trio, John Smith and Anthony Vaughan, were still alive in the mid-1800s when the Truro Company resumed work on the Island. At that time, the local newspapers ran stories about the discovery and the initial searches. It should be noted that Jotham B. McCully states that his 1849 search group (The Truro Company) resulted from a few people having heard the story from Simeon Lynds.

From the corroborated statements, it is not difficult to accept that there was, in fact, a clearing. The Pit was at least seven feet in diameter and over 110 deep. No less then 150 cubic yards of soil plus some from the flood tunnel was removed during the original work. On a project of that magnitude, it would have been necessary to clear away an area in order to pile the soil and to make room to work.

Trees of Nova Scotia, published by the Department of Lands and Forests, states that Nova Scotia red oak are "fast-growing" and that "young trees sprout vigorously when the stem is killed by fire or cutting."

According to the Extension Services Division of the Nova Scotia Department of Natural Resources, a Nova Scotia red oak with a diameter of between six and eight inches would probably be between 40 and 50 years old on Oak Island's type of soil. From my more than 30 years experience engineering and surveying in wooded areas of Nova Scotia, I believe that this is the maximum size of tree that could have been found growing in the clearing in 1795. I don't think that the clearing would have been noticed if the trees had been any larger. However, at this size or smaller, they would have contrasted against a more mature stand surrounding the clearing.

Edmund S. Telfer, Research Scientist with Environment Canada and a forester of long experience, was born, brought up and educated in southern Nova Scotia. Telfer was consulted on the probable length of elapsed time before the clearing would have become unrecognizable. Telfer recalls a farm field in his home village becoming a forest in the period of 30 years and in view of the type of drumlin (oval shaped hill of glacial drift) overburden on Oak Island, he contends that a clearing made in the period of 1575 (plus or minus 85 years) would have most certainly been regrowthed and obliterated by 1795. A field adjacent to my homestead in another part of the province was similarly regrowthed by maple and birch trees over a period of 30 years. Its state of maturity was such that if it were placed like a piece of a jigsaw puzzle into a fully mature forest it would only be marginally recognized as a clearing in a state of reforestation. After considering our observations, Telfer and I concurred that the clearing on Oak Island would unlikely have been more than 50 years old and more probably had been there in the vicinity of 30 years when it was discovered.

I found my first hint as to who might have carried out the Money Pit project during the period deduced from the early accounts in Thomas H. Raddall's *Halifax, Warden of the North*. In this book of the history of Halifax, Raddall writes about a "wild visitation from the south" following the British invasion of Havana in 1762. According to Raddall, the British fleet and army that captured Havana, Cuba, "with its enormous loot," arrived in Halifax and a wild spending spree and party took place while the ships remained moored in the harbor for a winter. Raddall writes: "There followed a saturnalia as this rabble of gaunt sunburned adventurers (Gorham's Rangers were among them) flung their pistareens, pieces of eight, and doubloons over the tavern bars and into the laps of the prostitutes." I was struck by Raddall's statement that the dissipation "was something beyond belief. The prize money distributed among so many soldiers and sailors was worth 400,000 pounds sterling, which they almost threw away. The birds of prey drawn here from all quarters by the hope of plunder made Halifax more like a pirates' rendezvous than a modest British settlement."

The British capture of Havana in 1762 receives little attention in general histories. Basically forgotten, it was a secret campaign conducted during the Seven Years' War and overshadowed by battles that decided the destiny of empires. Fortunately, a collection of notes, orders, directives and communiques covering the undertaking was printed for the Naval Records Society. (An organization founded for the purpose of printing rare or unpublished works of naval interest.) The clues and evidence found in this publication along with other sources strongly suggest a link with the legendary treasure of Oak Island.

On January 4, 1762, Britain declared war against Spain with the intent of attacking the Spanish empire. The British were retaliating against Spain joining forces with France during the Seven Years' War (1756–1763) which had involved all of the great powers of Europe.

Two days after the declaration of war, the British Cabinet met and approved a secret invasion and occupation of Havana, the center of Spanish power in the Caribbean, which was to be followed by an attack on Louisiana and Manila.

The motives behind the campaign were that Havana had a good harbor, it was the strongest naval base in the Caribbean, and according to British Intelligence, it was extremely rich in booty. Havana, a Spanish stronghold since 1511 and the dwelling place of many wealthy noblemen and ecclesiastics, was the communication link with the old world. It was also the supply port where convoys of Spanish galleons assembled from Caribbean ports for the overseas voyage to Spain, carrying millions of dollars worth of gold and silver. Here, rich cargoes were distributed among galleons, transferred from one ship to another, or stored to lighten overloaded vessels prior to their trans-Atlantic crossings.

It is not known who was responsible for dreaming up the plan but King George III (1738–1820) who ascended to the throne on the death of his Grandfather, George II, in 1760, shared a common interest with his uncle William Augustus, Duke of Cumberland (1721–1765), and John Stuart, third Earle of Bute (1713–1792), who was the young King's constant companion and adviser.

The King's zeal for the capture of Havana is indicated in a letter to Bute, dated January 6, 1762, in which he writes: "It gives me no small

King George III, ruler of Britain, during the sacking of Havana.

satisfaction that Cuba, Louisiane [sic], and the Manillas seem to be agreed on by those who assembl'd to day [sic]...." Indeed, the King had a lot to gain from a successful outcome.

George III began his reign determined to regain many lost powers of the monarchy. He expressed an unwillingness to abrogate power that he believed belonged to him and struggled to recover his royal rights. Between 1714 and 1760 the monarchy had been incapable of ruling without the support of parliament since the first two Georges (George I and George II) had been foreigners and their rights had been contested. The Crown was weak and that circumstance increased the power and importance of its supporters. British affairs were controlled by a party glued together by military and family connections, strengthened by corrupt practices such as bribery. Basically, political power was vested in a few noble families while the Crown was rapidly deteriorating into a mere figurehead without authority. But George was dedicated to changing the structure of power and resolved not to be governed by his ministers.

The expedition to capture Havana set sail on March 5, 1762, with Lieutenant-General George Keppel, Earl of Albemarle (1724–1772), in command of land forces, Sir George Pocock (1706–1792) in command of the Navy, and George Keppel's brother, Augustus (1725–1786), second in command under Pocock. The fleet reached Martinique on April 26th where the force was reembarked and reorganized and 600 Negro slaves were gathered up from various islands of the Lesser Antilles. The fleet left Martinique on May 6th, took the dangerous reef-ridden but shorter route along the north coast of Cuba and reached Havana on June 6th with an overwhelming naval and military force of about 200 ships and 11,000 troops.

Their arrival was a complete surprise. The Governor of Cuba and other Spanish officials were in church taking Mass when the fleet approached Havana. When they were told of the presence of a large squadron they assumed it was a friendly convoy, or ships "merely in passage."

Although the Spanish were caught off guard, the strong fortifications protecting Havana made the city almost impregnable and the attack resulted in a two-month siege which might have failed if it had not been aided towards the end by the arrival of 3,188 additional troops from

Admiral Pocock, in charge of the British navy during the siege of Havana, 1762.

Lt.-Gen. George Kappel, in charge of the British army during the siege, conspirator with Pocock.

Commodore Augustus Keppel, co-conspirator with his brother George.

New York. The undertaking ended with the surrender of Havana on August 12, 1762. Two days later, the British officially took possession of Havana including public moneys, city warehouses with their contents, public records, military equipment, and a dozen Spanish warships plus smaller vessels in the harbor. The British occupied Havana until July of the following year when it was returned to Spain in exchange for the Floridas, after the Peace of Paris went into effect.

During the term of rule, the British plundered Havana of its vast riches and extracted huge quantities of gold and silver from the Catholic Church and the many noblemen who dwelt in the city. The amount of wealth taken from Havana is subject to conjecture but it must have been mind-boggling. The quantity of gold and silver that had been produced in the New World (plunder of the Indian empires not included) is estimated in the billions of dollars. At the end of the colonial period the annual output was ten times the production of all the rest of the world. And it all went through Havana!

Entrance to Havana Harbor, 1762.

The captured Spanish Fleet.

The enormous cache from the Catholic Church can only be left to the imagination. The Bishop was banished to Florida but he must have counted the losses when Havana was returned. It is likely that the accumulated riches of the Church might have been a source of embarrassment to be kept secret, and the total loss undisclosed. Religious devotion waned in Latin America after the 16th century as institutionalism triumphed. The church became rich in silver and gold as thousands of churches and hundreds of converts and monasteries sprouted in the New World. With generous tax exemptions and the willing and granting of fortunes by the faithful, it was inevitable that the Church should amass considerable wealth. The Church in Latin America was a prosperous enterprise and the wealth of the powerful clergy can only be imagined.

The division of the booty was ordered in a letter (only a copy exists) dated February 18, 1762, in the King's name, from the Admiralty to Sir George Pocock. The directions specify that the booty from the expedition be distributed between the sea and land forces and that George Keppel, the Earl of Albemarle, settle with Pocock on the manner and proportion of distribution.

Not surprisingly, prior to landing in Cuba, Albemarle and Pocock drew up an agreement that provided generously for themselves. They stipulated that one-third of the whole be equally divided between them. Of the balance, one-fifteenth was to be divided equally between the second in command of the army and navy (Lieutenant-General Elliott and Admiral Augustus Keppel) and the remainder divided up on a descending order according to rank.

It appears from the February 18th directive that a settlement involving total distribution of all booty to the forces was uncommon and required substantiation. A promise is made by the Admiralty to provide two copies of former regulations "in order that Lord [Earl] Albemarle may be apprized of such methods as have been heretofore taken in like cases"[1] and discusses two past ventures to which the regulations pertain. The first was a combined British and Spanish invasion of Domingue in 1695 and the second a plan formulated in 1702 for a combined British and Dutch attack on Martinique or Havana. A further promise by the Admiralty is given to provide a paper prepared in 1740 conforming to the terms of the two former regulations.

---

[1] Quote from February 18, 1762 letter from Admiralty to Sir George Pocock.

The sincerity of the directive becomes more tarnished when at the end it orders a share of the plunder be given to the negro slaves as well as the regular troops.

Where was the Crown's share? It seems strange that the King would pass by the opportunity to demand some of the booty unless secret arrangements had been made with the navy and military commanders to place a portion in "safe keeping."

Could Albemarle and Pocock have arranged to siphon off a shipload or two of booty for additional commissions? From what is known of Albemarle, the answer is, quite possibly, yes! He was accused of being a greedy man. He apparently wasn't satisfied with his share of the prizes and tried to force several illegal taxes on British and American merchants. His conduct resulted in a long series of disputes and law suits.

It might be considered rather ridiculous to suggest that the King could have been involved in a secret operation involving help from the navy and army. It makes more sense, however, that it could have been a small clique composed of the King and a few of his key people and perhaps one or two of their loyal subordinates. The primary indication of such an exclusive circle is found in the biography of George Keppel, the Earl of Albemarle.

There is no apparent reason why Albemarle was selected to command the land forces in the Havana campaign. He had never held an important command and his military career had been without distinction. Furthermore, he was not imaginative or particularly quick-witted. He was, however, secretary and political representative to the King's uncle, the Duke of Cumberland. As well as once being the Duke's favorite aide-de-camp he had also been aide-de camp to King George II. He had also apparently been a confidant of Sir Jeffrey Amherst (1717–1797), Commander-in-Chief of the Army in North America who as a young man was aide-de-camp to General John Ligonier (Earl Ligonier, 1680–1770), later served on the Duke of Cumberland's staff, and still later assisted the Havana campaign. Among several letters to Amherst, Albemarle begins with: "Dear Jeff, It [sic] is very strange to me to write to Your Excellency in a formal way...." He ends the letter with a postscript saying: "Pray send me some money, I have none...." and blames his empty pockets on a loan of 10,000 pounds made to Major-General the Honorable Robert Monckton. Wolfe, the famous British army commander called Albemarle, "one of those showy men who are seen in palaces and in the courts of men.... He desires never to see his regiment and wishes that no officer would ever leave it." Albemarle may have been the strongest driving force behind the campaign for it has often been said that "the expedition was undertaken solely to put money into the Keppels' pockets."

Commodore Augustus Keppel (brother of George Keppel, the Earl of Albemarle), second in command under Sir George Keppel during the Havana expedition, also had a rather lackluster military record. On June 27, 1747, he totally wrecked the 50-gun *Maidstone*, of which he was in command, when he ran her aground while chasing an enemy ship off Belle Isle in the Bay of Biscay, France. He and his men were taken prisoners. Keppel was released to the British on exchange and was tried by court-martial. Probably through the influence of his brother George, he was honorably acquitted.

Another probable member of the suggested clique was Lord Anson (George Anson, 1697–1762), the First Lord of the Admiralty, who, with the assistance of the previously mentioned General Ligonier, is thought to have been the key planner and organizer of the campaign. Like the others, Lord Anson's enthusiasm for the operation was undoubtedly fueled by the expectation of plunder. In June 1743 while serving in the Pacific in command of the *Centurion*, Anson captured a great Spanish galleon which made annual voyages between Manila and Acapulco. The amount of booty was enormous and when the *Centurion* returned to England in June 1744, the treasure was paraded through the streets of London on 32 wagons accompanied by the ship's crew, marching with colors and to the music of a naval band. Among his crew members was no other than Augustus Keppel (later Commodore Keppel, second in command of the naval force in the Havana expedition).

The Duke of Cumberland may have subtly been at the apex of his Majesty's suspected clique. Significantly, through his power as captain-general and the only surviving son of George II, he successfully obtained a ruling in 1751 that gave him sole responsibility for filling military posts. He thus "plucked a very useful feather out of the cap of the ministry." This gave the Duke great power in organizing an operation because he could pick his favorites.

The Duke of Cumberland was no doubt a strong supporter of his nephew's (King George III) drive for power. His nephew treated him

The Duke of Cumberland who chose the players in the clique that sacked Havana and took control of its immense wealth.

with respect and consideration and he in turn provided advice and assistance to his nephew who strove to regain his royal rights.

The Duke of Cumberland's interest in the campaign is indicated in a letter of 1762 to the Earl of Albemarle in which he wrote: "No joy can equal mine, and I strut and plume myself as if it was I that had taken the Havannah [old English name for Havana]."

When the Duke died suddenly on October 31, 1765, Albemarle was appointed administer to his estate since the Duke was unmarried, and left no will.

The theory of a clandestine operation is strengthened by evidence of an enormous discrepancy in the amount of booty officially reported and that determined from other sources. According to information provided from a private search conducted in Spanish archives in 1977 and translated into English, the value of the plunder amounted to many millions of British pounds. This information is further supported in a biography of Admiral Keppel which places the prize money upwards of three million. We also learn from the private search that in the immediate months following the surrender of Havana, Spanish galleons loaded with gold and silver, with commanders who knew nothing of the secret invasion, sailed into Havana Harbor and were taken by the occupying British.

The quantity of many millions of pounds seems credible but is contrary to a March 7, 1772, document by Pocock giving a general account of all receipts and payments and ultimate distribution of prize money which indicates that only 737,000 pounds had been turned over to the Havana captors.

During the ten-month occupation of Havana, the British navy and army commanders had a splendid opportunity to remove and conceal a large portion of booty. The Earl of Albemarle and Sir George Pocock were more or less completely in charge of their respective affairs. Within acceptable limits to the Admiralty, they could prolong their tenures and depart when they saw fit.

In a letter dated October 9, 1762, Pocock gave John Clevland, First Secretary to the Board of Admiralty, an update on events and made his and Albemarle's proposals. In this letter Pocock said that all the ships except three would depart before the beginning of November and, of those, a portion would go to Jamaica under Admiral Augustus Keppel. Stating his intention to depart later in the month with 60 ships, he reported that Albemarle proposed to leave independently towards the end of December. As to what had already taken place, Pocock informed Clevland, among various matters, that three war ships had been dispatched to Halifax, Nova Scotia, in response to news from New York and Boston that the French had invaded Newfoundland.

With such freedom of movement, there seems to have been ample opportunity to conceal treasure in a previously prepared location.

Given the noted discrepancy between the estimated treasure seized and that reported, the waiving of a portion of the plunder by the Crown, the freedom of movement, the time-frame corresponding to the deduced age of the Money Pit, and the nature of his Majesty's clique, I suggest that there is plausible connection between the sacking of Havana and Oak Island. This is how I see it.

A British warship slips into Mahone Bay in the spring of 1762 and follows a precharted course to a point of land that looks like a jut of the mainland but is shown on the chart as an island. On board is an engineer and his work crew, along with a small contingency of soldiers to stand guard over whatever project is about to be carried out. The mission is a military secret.

The engineer carries a package of secret military documents which are in the form of plans and specifications for the construction of a subterranean complex of storage chambers and watertight vaults. The engineer surmises that what he is about to build is an ammunition storage facility. The project makes very good sense considering its proximity to the Halifax garrison.

The engineering core and the military guard will overwinter on the island and complete the project by late spring or early summer of the following year. Provisions will be shipped in as needed.

The warship sails away and the engineer and his crew set to work while the guard watches for intruders. The township of Shoreham (Chester) was formed three years earlier and although it is only in its infancy, precaution is essential. Although the subject island is hidden from Shoreham by other islands, someone might see the project from an elevated position and come to investigate or a fisherman might suddenly appear.

A deep shaft is sunk near the top of the hill between the north and south coves, tunnels are fingered out from various levels and storage chambers are constructed reflecting the prudent decision not to put all the eggs in one basket. Finally, work is started on a complex flood system to make the recovery of the treasure impossible by an enemy.

Down south, in Havana, the siege is over. A large British ship receives a mother lode of plunder and prepares to set sail for England. The ship is commanded by George Keppel, the Earl of Albemarle, with a new captain and crew who were not in Cuba harbor when the ship was loaded. The original crew were also absent when Albemarle's ship received her spoils of war; they had been whisked off to New York only a few days following the British victory.

On departure, the captain asks Albemarle what the wooden boxes in the hold contain as the ship handles as if loaded with an abnormally heavy cargo. Albemarle replies that the cargo is ammunition left over from the siege—canon balls and other heavy artillery—bound for a secret military location.

It is a simple but well executed plan. Somewhere north of Bermuda, Albemarle orders his ship's captain to strike a course for Nova Scotia and hands him a paper giving the latitude and longitude of Mahone Bay. He tells the captain that the military equipment on board will be stowed in a secret ammunition magazine, close to the Halifax garrison. Its location is a top secret. The crew are to be told nothing about the nature of the cargo or its location, and the captain is ordered not to divulge its whereabouts to a living soul—the security of England's position in the New World hinges on it. The captain is honored to be trusted with such an important assignment and vows to take the secret to his grave.

In mid December 1762 Albemarle's ship drops anchor off of Oak Island. Almost everything is ready except the completion of the construction of the artificial beach of the flood system and the engineer takes Albemarle on a tour of the project.

The ship's crew unload the wooden boxes and Albemarle directs the operation of placement while the engineer and his crew continue with their work on the artificial beach. The ship's dunnage which was discarded on the shore during the unloading of the supposed ammunition is utilized and spread over the previously laid eel grass.

The engineer has made a detailed survey and placed the appropriate markers as called for in the specifications. Following the instructions of specifications, he folds and seals all the documents including his plan of survey and addresses them to "His Majesty the King" and personally hands them over to Albemarle.

The ship departs, the artificial beach is completed, the deep shaft is backfilled and the flood system is activated. Then the men break camp and clean up the site. A broken wrought iron stove of the type used in a ship's captain's cabin is buried in a shallow hole and covered over during the placement of the large cone-shaped stone survey markers.

Meanwhile, Albemarle arrives in England, more or less on schedule, since he had only "proposed" to depart Havana near the end of December.

One stone remains unturned: why didn't anyone return for the treasure? I suggest that the answer is found in King George's struggle for power and the condition of his health. When the Havana campaign was planned, King George was undoubtedly anticipating the day when his power over the military would be absolute. In 1806, following the death of William Pitt, leading minister of parliament, George requested that the Army be under the direct control of the Crown. Incoming ministers defeated his bid for greater power. A compromise was reached whereby no changes in the Army would be introduced without his approval. Therefore, it is not unreasonable to assume that King George was waiting until he had complete control over the Oak Island operation, before initiating the treasure's recovery. He procrastinated. The years slipped by and then it was too late. He lost his mind and then he died.

There is historical documentation to suggest that King George's health problems are to blame for his failure to recover the riches. On January 12, 1765, George was attacked by a severe illness in the nature of a bad chest cold. It was serious and persisted intermittently for three months. Symptoms of mental derangement appeared during this illness and for the balance of his life he suffered from what has been recently diagnosed from his lengthy medical records as "acute intermittent porphyria," an illness marked by mental aberrations, hallucinations, and delusions. George suffered from the disease on five major occasions with frequent incidents of lesser severity, described as "periods of flurry."

Towards the end of 1810, George began to show signs of permanent derangement of mind. In the last ten years of his life the disease rendered him senile, blind and, towards the end, deaf. George was placed in regency under the Queen in 1811, since he was no longer able to perform his function as monarch. He died on January 29, 1820.

Today, while we armchair treasure hunters deduce new theories or find facts to better support existing ones, the search on Oak Island continues. Fred Nolan backs his pickup truck down to the shore of Crandall's Point and unloads his aluminum boat. It is 9:00 a.m. on a warm sunny Saturday morning and he has a hunch that this will be his lucky day. As he secures the outboard motor to the stern, a car drives across the causeway and stops at the nearby locked gate. Dan Blankenship steps out and quickly unlocks and opens the gate to let in a carload of tourists. Both men pretend not to notice the other's presence.

An hour later, Nolan drives his backhoe to a spot where two survey lines intersect. He will dig here today. He has always believed that there is a large treasure close to the ground surface. Perhaps only ten or twenty feet below he will strike the jackpot. And while he digs, Blankenship takes a moment to watch from the dirt road that skirts the shore. He wonders, what is Nolan up to today? But there is little time to dally. Five bus loads of people are scheduled to visit the Money Pit today and he's the guide. And there is no rest for the weary. On Monday he'll be busy setting up the drilling rig in a new location. The treasure hunt goes on.

Epilogue

On March 23, 1993, after submitting the final draft of *Oak Island Gold* to my publisher, I received a newspaper clipping from a friend with whom I had discussed the Havana theory. It was an article dated September 9, 1991 and entitled "Mosher Treasures Oak Island Memories" by Nadine Fowness of the South Shore Bureau of the Halifax Herald Ltd.

In this article, Mr. Carl Mosher, who is now 81 and living at the veterans unit of Fishermen's Memorial Hospital in Lunenburg, recalls the day his grandmother, Lucy Vaughan, gestured to him to follow her upstairs to his grandparents' bedroom at their Western Shore home. "I was only 13 or 14 years of age and my grandmother, Lucy Vaughan, called me aside and took me into the bedroom. She opened up a wooden trunk and in it was a bunch of bags—all kinds of nice white bags tied at the top with blue string. My grandfather, George Vaughan, told me he got that chest off of Oak Island. He lived right across from it," Mr. Mosher reminisced.

Mr. Mosher said that he was too young at the time to take much interest in what the white bags contained but he presumes that they were filled with gold since they were from Oak Island.

Like the legendary maps of Oak Island, the whereabouts of the chest and its contents is now unknown, but Mr. Mosher had this to say about its disappearance: "My uncle, Edward Vaughan, knew about the chest. He got a hold of it and left everything else he had here go—his property, his business, his wife, and family. No one heard from him for years and then a few years back we heard he died a pauper somewhere up in Toronto."

To follow up, I interviewed Mr. Mosher on April 7, 1993. Except for being confined to a wheelchair, Mr. Mosher appeared to be in good health and of sound mind. He reminisced about the Chappell's expedition of the early 1930s, recalling details of the Chappell shaft on which he had worked as both a hoist operator and a driller.

The conversation turned to that day of 68 or 69 years ago when his grandmother showed him the contents of the chest. His story was identical to that of the *Halifax Herald* article, embellished with details. He estimated that the bags had been eight to ten inches in diameter and ten to twelve inches deep. I asked him how many bags there were in the chest and he said, "I imagine there was 25 or more and they were all equalled up pretty well." He said he lifted one out and it was heavy. It was tied with a draw-string that had a "bow-tie tied onto it."

I asked Mr. Mosher if he had seen the contents of the bags and he said no. Then I asked him why he hadn't asked his grandmother to let him take a peek inside a bag and he said, "I was only about 13 at the time. My grandmother knew it...that there was gold in the bags. That's why she showed them to me." He said that if he had *wanted* to examine the contents of one of the bags, he could well have asked. "I could have had one of those bags if I had wanted it," he explained. "If I had asked my grandfather for one, he would have given it to me."

Looking back over the years, Mr. Mosher is still certain that the bags contained gold. He remarked there had been an unexplained jump in his grandfather's financial status. Before he died, he set his son Edward up with a sawmill and a blacksmith shop, and he seems to have been well off in his later years, in contrast to his status as a younger man. Mosher reports, "I heard my grandfather say that when he got married, he had to borrow money for flour to make the first loaf of bread."

Although the suggestion of a chest of treasure in George and Lucy Vaughan's bedroom may raise the odd eyebrow, Carl Mosher and his wife Hilda have a long-standing connection with Oak Island. Hilda is the granddaughter of Sophia Sellers—daughter of Anthony Graves who owned most of the Island and who is rumored to have used Spanish money to stock his kitchen cupboards. Carl's mother's side is related to the Vaughans that settled on the mainland across from the Island who were involved in the Money Pit discovery and subsequent searches.

Some investigators believe that although the mother lode of treasure remains intact, there was and still may be some loose change lying around. They theorize that a few chests of treasure were cached in shallow pits about the Island, apart from the Money Pit. If true, this could explain the chest in George and Lucy's bedroom.

I would have relegated this newspaper clipping to a forgotten file drawer, had it not been for one seemingly insignificant bit of information arising out of the research I had done on the Siege of Havana.

When the British finally succeeded in storming the Spanish fortress, a huge pile of treasure awaited them. Apparently, the Spanish had been preparing to somehow sneak it out the back door just before the British came clambering over the walls. There, on the floor of the fortress plaza, were stacked 178 chests, each holding 20 white canvas bags, filled with gold!

Bibliography

Ayling, Stanley, *George the Third*. London, William Collins Sons & Co. Ltd. 1972.

Baigent, Michael; Leigh, Richard and Lincoln, Henry, *The Holy Blood and the Holy Grail*. London, Transworld Publishers Ltd., 1990.

Bird, Will R., *Off-Trail in Nova Scotia*. Toronto, The Ryerson Press, 1956.

Bradley, Michael, *Holy Grail Across the Atlantic: The Secret History of Canadian Discovery and Exploration*. Willowdale, Ontario, Hounslow Press, 1988.

Burns, E. Bradford, *Latin America: A Concise Interpretive History*. New Jersey, Prentice-Hall, Inc., 1972.

Clarke, George Frederick, *Expulsion of the Acadians: The True Story*. Fredericton, New Brunswick, Brunswick Press, 1980.

Creighton, Helen, *Bluenose Ghosts*. Toronto, McGraw-Hill Ryerson Ltd., 1957.

Creighton, Helen, *Bluenose Magic*. Toronto, McGraw-Hill Ryerson Ltd., 1968.

Creighton, Helen, *Folklore of Lunenburg County, Nova Scotia*. Toronto, McGraw-Hill Ryerson Ltd., 1976.

Crooker, William S., *The Oak Island Quest*. Windsor, Nova Scotia, Lancelot Press, 1978.

Crow, John A., *The Epic of Latin America*. New York, Doubleday & Company, Inc., 1971.

Department of Lands and Forests, *Trees of Nova Scotia: A Guide to the Native and Exotic Species*. Halifax (?), 1970.

DesBrisay, M.B., *History of the County of Lunenburg*. The Bridgewater Bulletin Ltd., 1967.

Dictionary of National Biography. London, Smith Elder & Co., England.

Driscoll, Charles B., *Doubloons*. New York, Farrar & Rinehart, Inc., 1930.

Earle, Peter, *The Treasure of the Conception*. New York, Viking Press, 1980.

Fredea, Josephine, "The Lure of Pirate's Gold." *Collier's Weekly*, 1905.

Furneaux, Rupert, *Fact, Fake or Fable.* London, Cassell and Company Limited, 1954.

Furneaux, Rupert, *Money Pit: The Mystery of Oak Island*. Great Britain, 1972.

Freidel, Frank, *Franklin D. Roosevelt, The Apprenticeship*. Boston, Little Brown and Company, 1952.

Halifax Herald Limited (The *Chronicle-Herald* and the *Mail-Star*), Halifax. Various articles on Oak Island.

Harris Reginald V., *The Oak Island Mystery*. Toronto, The Ryerson Press, 1967.

Herring, Hubert, *A History of Latin America: From the Beginning to the Present*. New York, Alfred A. Knopf, 1955.

Mowat, Farley, *West Viking*. Toronto, McClelland and Stewart Limited, 1965.

Namier, Sir Lewis, *The Structure of Politics at the Accession of George III*. New York, MacMillan & Co. Ltd., 1968.

O'Connor, D'Arcy, *The Money Pit*. New York, Coward, McCann & Geoghegan, Inc, 1978.

O'Connor, D'Arcy, *The Big Dig*. New York, Ballantine Books, 1988.

MacDonald, David, Oak Island's Mysterious "Money Pit." *Readers Digest*, January 1965. Condensed from the Rotarian.

McKendrick, Melvennä, *The Horizon Concise History of Spain*. New York, American Heritage Publishing Co., Inc., 1972.

McLellan, J.S., *Louisbourg from Its Foundation to Its Fall, 1713–1758*. Sydney, Nova Scotia, Fortress Press, 1969.

McLeod, Carol, *Captain William Kidd: Scapegoat or Scoundrel*. Antigonish, Nova Scotia, Formac Publishing Company Limited, 1979.

Raddall, Thomas H., *Halifax, Warden of the North*. New York, Doubleday & Company, Inc, 1965.

Ritchie, Robert C., *Captain Kidd and the War Against Pirates*. Cambridge, Massachusetts, Harvard University Press, 1986.

Snow, Edward Rowe, *True Tales of Buried Treasure*. New York, Dodd, Mead & Company, 1062.

Syrett, David, *The Siege and Capture of Havana, 1762*. The Navy Records Society, London and Colchester, 1970.

Urdang, Lawrence Associates, *Lives of the Georgian Age, 1714–1837*. New York, Harper & Row Publishers, Inc., 1978.

Ward, Geoffrey, C., *Before the Trumpet: Young Franklin Roosevelt, 1882–1905*. New York, Harper & Row, Publishers, 1985.

Wells, G.H., *The Outlines of History*. New York, Doubleday & Company, Inc., 1961.

Whitehead, Ruth Holmes, *The Old Man Told Us*. Halifax, Nova Scotia, Nimbus Publishing Limited, 1991.

Winston Alexander, *No Man Knows My Grave: Privateers and Pirates, 1665–1715*. Boston, Houghton Mifflin Company, 1969.

Young, George, *Ancient People and Modern Ghosts*. Queensland, Nova Scotia, George Young, 1980.